QUEEN ELIZABETH II
—
A BIRTHDAY TRIBUTE

QUEEN ELIZABETH II
—
A BIRTHDAY TRIBUTE

Foreword by
The Earl of Lichfield

St Michael

CONTENTS

Text by Judy Todd

First published in 1985 exclusively for
Marks and Spencer p.l.c., Baker Street, London,
by Newnes Books,
a division of The Hamlyn Publishing Group Limited,
84–88 The Centre, Feltham, Middlesex, TW13 4BH.

Copyright © Newnes Books 1985

ISBN 0 600 35895 X

Printed in Italy.

FOREWORD

This book is a sixtieth birthday tribute to our Queen.
Since her birth on April 21, 1926 her life has been
interwoven with events great and small in Britain and
the Commonwealth. It is interesting to note that from
a very early age – long before it was thought that she
would one day be Queen – the public had a special
affection for her. As events placed her more and more
in the limelight, this affection could only grow,
coupled with great admiration for her unstinting
devotion to duty.

When making the selection of photographs for this
book, I was struck again and again by the depth and
range of the Queen's role. The thought constantly in
mind is how does she do it – the innumerable tours,
state occasions, and the happy family events? She
remains always the charming, capable and consistent
figurehead, but an appealingly human one.

It comes across so clearly that the Queen's strength is
based on her family life. While other members of this
fascinating family receive much press attention –
most recently the Prince and Princess of Wales – it is
still the Queen who is head of the family, the nation
and the Commonwealth. This record of those years
acknowledges our gratitude and affection.

THE RT HON THE EARL OF LICHFIELD FBIPP FRPS

THE YOUNG PRINCESS

A diminutive figure as she follows in the footsteps of her grandmother, Princess Elizabeth nevertheless manages to emulate her regal bearing as she and her sister are welcomed to the 1934 Braemar Gathering near Balmoral.

As the young Duchess of York proudly held her firstborn for the benefit of the official photographer after the Christening on 29 May 1926 there can have been few of those present who dreamt that they were looking on the face destined to become the most photographed in the world. That is not to say that interest in this tiny Princess was lacking. In fact, it was intense. She was old King George V's first grand-daughter and the first of a new royal generation. But her father, Prince Albert, was only the King's second son. The dashing older brother – David, as he was then known – was not yet thirty-two and would undoubtedly marry and have an heir in time. The attention of the world's media would switch to him or her, leaving the Yorks to get on quietly with their own lives.

The twenty-five-year-old Duchess was the second youngest of Lord and Lady Strathmore's ten children and descended from one of Scotland's noble families, the Bowes-Lyons, whose seat had been Glamis Castle since the middle of the fourteenth century. A strikingly attractive girl with immense charm and an easy way with everyone, she soon caught the attention of Prince Albert. The romance began after the Lady Elizabeth Bowes-Lyon, then staying at her parents' London home, became friendly with the King's daughter, Princess Mary, through their shared interest in the Girl Guide Movement. She was taken to the Palace to meet the Princess's family, and her friendship with the daughter so deepened that in 1922 when the Princess married Viscount Lascelles it seemed only natural that the Lady Elizabeth should attend her friend as bridesmaid.

Below Proud parents with baby Elizabeth Alexandra Mary at Buckingham Palace in May 1926.

Opposite Glamis Castle near Dundee, picturesque home of the Strathmore family since 1372. Prince Albert visited his future bride here and

their young daughter spent her first summer at the castle.

Opposite, inset The Drawing Room or Great Hall, where the Duke and Duchess of York and their young family must have spent many a happy hour.

Prince Albert meanwhile was continuing with his naval service but in his spare time seeing a lot of the Strathmore family, occasionally hunting on their Scottish estates or journeying down to stay with them at their red-brick English country home, St Paul's Walden Bury in Hertfordshire. Lord Strathmore was a kindly, but retiring, man; it was his wife, an artistic and well-informed lady full of enthusiasm for everything around her, who was largely responsible for creating the friendly and stimulating atmosphere in the Strathmore homes. Prince Albert was totally captivated by it all, and especially by the youngest daughter. He was not the only one, however, and must have watched nervously as others paid their attentions to the vivacious and talented Elizabeth. A shy young man with a stammer, an appalling handicap for one in his position, he was only too relieved that he had a flamboyant older brother into whose shadow he could quietly disappear. None of his family

Above **Prince Albert, Duke of York, with his bride, the former Lady Elizabeth Bowes-Lyon, on their wedding day, 26 April 1923. Next to the new Duchess are her parents, the Earl and Countess of Strathmore. Seated beside the King, Queen Mary looks equally splendid.**

Right **A happy honeymoon photograph of the Duke and Duchess of York, taken in the grounds of Polesden Lacey, the country house near Dorking in Surrey which was lent to them by Mrs Ronald Greville. The rest of the honeymoon was spent at Glamis**

doubted that he needed a good wife to boost his confidence and ensure that his qualities were not undervalued. When Prince Albert announced his intentions to his parents there was certainly no doubt in their minds that Elizabeth would be such a wife.

It seemed for a while as if the Prince must seek his happiness elsewhere, for his first proposal was rejected. The Lady Elizabeth hesitated, reluctant to have her life cast into the spotlight which must inevitably fall even on retiring members of Britain's First Family. But the Prince was very determined, and finally, early in 1923, while they walked in the woods at St Paul's, the lady relented. In spite of the hesitations it was so obviously a love match that everyone was delighted. Newspapermen scurried around trying to discover more about the relatively unknown girl who was about to prove such a delightful addition to the Royal Family.

Once her mind was made up there was little time for the future Duchess of York to change it, for the wedding was arranged for 26 April 1923. It was a splendid affair at Westminster Abbey, with the groom attended by his brothers, the Prince of Wales and Prince Henry, and the bride by eight bridesmaids. As she entered the Abbey the Lady Elizabeth spontaneously laid her bouquet of white York roses and Scottish heather on the tomb of the Unknown Soldier, a tribute to her own two brothers killed in the First World War as well as to the nation's other fallen sons. Thus, with one of her last gestures as a commoner, she expressed that oneness with the people which was ever after to characterise her life of service.

Castle, the bride's childhood home, where she unromantically developed whooping cough.

Overleaf St Paul's Walden Bury, the Strathmores' Hertfordshire home. The baby Princess Elizabeth spent some of her earliest months here, staying with her maternal grandparents while the Duke and Duchess of York were away on their 1927 tour of Australia. She inherited her mother's old nursery and it was under the guidance of the Duchess's own nurse, Miss Knight, that she learnt to walk.

Nearly six centuries earlier it had been a male member of her family, John Lyon, chamberlain to Scotland's King David II, who at the height of a distinguished career had married the widowed sister of David's successor Robert II and thus founded the fortunes of the Lyon family, fortunes augmented in the eighteenth century by marriage into the rich Durham-based Bowes family. Now, the royal connection was being re-established by a female member who was quickly to endear herself to everyone. Even the usually gruff and austere King George melted in the presence of his new daughter-in-law.

For the first years of their marriage the couple lived at White Lodge in Richmond Park, a house with notable royal connections. Queen Mary had grown up in this mansion, and the Duke of Windsor was born here. Meanwhile, Prince Albert continued with his naval career, at the same time developing an interest in industrial relations. He found his new wife a great support and the couple enjoyed a large measure of personal popularity, not least because the Duchess seemed to bring a breath of fresh air into royal circles. It was generally a somewhat depressing time, for the great patriotism that had been aroused during the war had dissolved into a disillusion and despair which were to culminate in the General Strike.

That event was still some way off when it was announced that the Duchess was expecting her first baby in the spring of 1926. It was perhaps a tribute to the great affection that existed between Lady Strathmore and her daughter that the Duchess decided to 'go home to mother' to await this happy event. The wait proved longer than expected and King George grew particularly solicitous about his daughter-in-law's health. He was somewhat relieved to be told on 20 April that three doctors had been called to attend the Duchess at 17 Bruton Street. It was there, at 2.40 on the morning of 21 April 1926, that a fair-haired baby girl with blue eyes was delivered by Caesarian section.

Even the Princess's entry into the world was attended by some ceremony for in the next room waited Sir William Joynson-Hicks, Secretary of State for Home Affairs. He had been summoned in accordance with a custom instituted during the seventeenth century after suspicions that a child had been smuggled into the birth chamber in a warming pan to be passed off as royal offspring. Thereafter, whenever a child who might one day inherit the Crown made its entry into the world a Minister had to be present in the next room as a witness to the validity of the birth.

The baby is reported to have had only a yawn with which to greet this first of her many Ministers. News of her safe arrival was phoned through to Windsor, where the King was woken at four a.m. to be told. Naturally there was delight and relief for both grandparents, feelings soon to be shared throughout the land. First outside the family to be officially informed of the happy event was by tradition the Lord Mayor of London, and later in the morning his daughter was one of the first visitors to arrive, bearing in her arms a bouquet of flowers for the young mother. Preceding her, as the very first visitor, was that Princess Mary whose friendship had so transformed the Duchess's life. In the afternoon the King and Queen motored down from Windsor to congratulate their son and daughter-in-law and to admire the new baby, pronounced by Queen Mary to be 'a little darling'.

Gun salutes at the Tower and in Hyde Park duly signalled public rejoicing at the arrival of the third in line of succession, but few can have guessed how historic an event it would prove to be. Today 17 Bruton Street is no more. It was demolished in 1938 to make way for Berkeley Square House and a bank which bears on its walls a plaque of Welsh slate recording that Queen Elizabeth II was born in a house on this site.

In retrospect it seems an extraordinary stroke of Fate that at her christening six weeks later (through which she cried almost continuously) the baby was given a name associated with one of the most glorious periods of England's history, though it was also of course her mother's name. The other two names conferred on her by the Archbishop of York at the ceremony in Buckingham Palace's chapel were Alexandra and Mary, commemorating her great-grandmother, Edward VII's beautiful and much loved Danish queen, and her grandmother, that imposing royal lady who was one of the sponsors at the christening. Like many relations before and after her, Elizabeth was baptised in the golden Lily Font made for the christening of Queen Victoria's firstborn and specially brought from Windsor for the occasion. Inside it was water from the Holy Land, from that very River Jordan in which Christ himself was baptised.

Apart from this foray to Buckingham Palace for her christening the baby Elizabeth spent her first months at White Lodge, where people waited in hopes of a glimpse as she was taken out for an airing by her nanny. As well as the stares of complete strangers, the infant had to get used to travelling, for part of her first

Right **Reunited at last after six months' separation from their young daughter, the Duke and Duchess wave to the cheering crowds from the balcony of 145 Piccadilly after their return from the triumphant Australian tour on 28 June 1927. Elizabeth had been the first member of the family to move into the new home.**

Below **A charming family portrait taken by top photographer Marcus Adams. The little Princess started wearing jewellery at a very early age and her necklace is probably the strand of coral beads given to her by the Duchess as a special parting gift at Christmas 1926.**

summer was spent up at Glamis with her maternal grandparents. Then in the autumn it was back to London and her other grandparents at the Palace before setting off for Sandringham at Christmas.

If the little Princess's life was not exactly underprivileged, there was one early deprivation not suffered by most of her future subjects – the absence of her parents for six months early in her young life. On the other side of the world the people of Australia were busy building a new capital and wanted a representative of the King to open the first Canberra Parliament in May 1927. The Prince of Wales had only recently visited them, so the King's second son and his wife were chosen for the task. The air routes to Australia had not yet been opened up, so just getting there and back involved a two-month-long sea journey. It must have been a great sorrow for the Duchess in particular to think that she would miss seeing so much of her daughter's crucial development, but it was felt that Elizabeth, not yet a year old, was far too young for such an adventure.

Elizabeth spent the first three months of her parents' absence with Lady Strathmore at St Paul's Walden Bury. There she discovered her mother's old nursery, and under the guidance of the Duchess's own nurse, Miss Knight, or 'Allah' as she was known, the little Princess learnt to walk. It was here also that she was introduced to animals as pets, and in particular to two dogs – large chows.

Below **Warmly wrapped against the weather, Princess Elizabeth leaves 145 Piccadilly for a drive in the park in 1928. There was enormous public interest in the King's first grand-daughter and it seems that she very early on found an appropriate way of acknowledging it.**

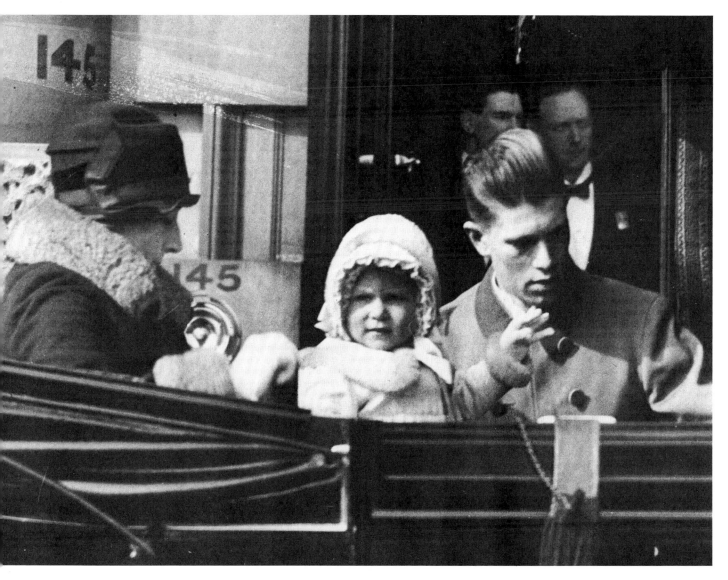

All the while her parents, 12,000 miles away, were receiving frequent reports of their daughter's progress, with a succession of photographs as evidence. They were also acquiring a mountain of presents to bring back home, too many in fact for one small girl to cope with single-handed, so that the bulk of them had to be dispatched to hospitals and children's homes.

Princess Elizabeth was nearly a year old when the first three months of her parents' absence were up and she had to return to London to stay with her other grandparents at Buckingham Palace. There she took another crucial step along the road from babyhood, learning to say 'Mummy' even in her mother's absence. She invented an ingenious variation on her own name, 'Lilibet', by which she was to be known for many years to come.

When the Yorks finally got back from their triumphant Australian tour there was a daughter waiting for them who must almost have seemed a stranger. There was also a new home, 145 Piccadilly, which had been acquired as a town house for the family before the parents left for their tour, but which only the little

Princess had as yet lived in. She had her own nursery on the top floor and there was a small garden at the back where she could play outdoors without attracting the attention attendant on every sortie in her pram into nearby Hyde Park. It was from this house that she was taken to Buckingham Palace on 27 June 1927 for what must have been a most touching family reunion.

The Duchess of York was now in a position to supervise her daughter's upbringing personally, which she insisted on doing most closely. Elizabeth learnt her ABC at her mother's knee, mastering the art of reading before she was six, and it was Mother who recited nursery rhymes with her and told her fairy tales.

Although a young child surrounded by adults, Elizabeth was not, while growing up, totally isolated from others of her own generation. Her cousins the Lascelles boys, sons of her mother's old friend the Princess Royal, came to tea with her at the Palace, and on her journeyings round the country to the various homes of her mother's youth she was introduced to many other cousins as well as to the children of her mother's friends.

Above **The Duchess of York with her mother, the Countess of Strathmore. There was a very strong bond between them and the Duchess went back to Glamis Castle for the birth of her second daughter on 21 August 1930.**

Left **Ponies were early favourites of the Princess, but she was equally capable of enjoying a ride through** the park on her tricycle under the usually watchful eyes of the ever-present nanny.

Below **Princess Elizabeth was a favourite of her grandfather George V. Here she is driving back with him and Queen Mary after attending Sunday morning service at Crathie church during the autumn holiday at Balmoral on Deeside in 1932.**

The youngest member of the family continued to be the delight of the ageing King, who felt tempted to spoil her in a way he had never spoilt his own children, with whom he had always been most aloof and strict. It was no surprise therefore that it was she who should have been invited to Bognor to help him recuperate from the serious illness that had attacked him at the end of 1928. He delighted in the youthful company and the Princess for her part developed a strong affection for the bearded 'Grandpapa England' who spent many long hours playing with her.

Soon, however, there was to be another object for the King's affection. It was announced that the Duchess was expecting her second child in the August of 1930. On the twenty-first day of that month the skies around Glamis were alight with the fires from beacons proclaiming to the people of Scotland the birth of another princess, to be christened Margaret Rose in a ceremony at Buckingham Palace the following month. From the first, hers was a welcome arrival. Here was a future playmate and companion for Elizabeth, one who would not be left behind as the family packed its bags and set off for another destination south or north of the Border.

Opposite **This charming tile picture gracing the walls of Ealing Hospital in London shows the two Princesses standing by the sundial in the garden of the little Welsh cottage at Royal Lodge, Windsor.**

Below **Even princesses can be tomboys. Young Margaret joins her older sister in some fun and games at the Abergeldie Castle Fete in 1933. The castle is close to Balmoral, the Royal Family's favourite Scottish retreat.**

In spite of their long sojourns in London, the Princesses were to grow up very much children of the open air and the country. The two Bowes-Lyon homes had plenty of open space around them in which to roam and there were acres of wild countryside at Balmoral. Now that their family had increased, the Yorks felt justified in having a house of their own in the country and were delighted when Royal Lodge in Windsor Great Park was offered to them by the King in 1932. After this originally Nash-designed house had been renovated and decorated, it made a very pleasant and secluded hideaway for the family where the Princesses could indulge their mutual passion for animals. Here they kept ponies, dogs, budgies, even two fawns, and it was in the park in the early morning that they could often be found out riding with their father. Elizabeth was already a competent horsewoman, having been given her first Shetland pony 'Peggy' before she was four and received her first lessons from Owen, the King's stud groom. The practice of such activities at so young an age was to serve her well in future life, as were the dancing lessons begun in 1931 and the French lessons given by a visiting French governess.

Above **Y Bwthyn Bach. 'The Little House' given to the Princess by the people of Wales. Although a sixth-birthday present, it was not actually erected in the gardens of the Royal Lodge at Windsor until 1936. Years later film of Peter Phillips playing in the house, with his grandmother the Queen watching, would delight television viewers.**

Opposite, top **King George V's health was obviously declining when this picture was taken but he and Queen Mary seem happy to pose with their beloved grand-daughters and daughter-in-law outside the miniature Welsh cottage.**

Opposite, bottom **Rapt attention from all the family during a visit to the circus at Olympia in 1935. The royal children and their parents shared the British passion for animals.**

Fortunately Princess Elizabeth was a quick learner, as the lady who arrived to be her governess in October 1933 was to find out. Marion Crawford, or 'Crawfie' as she was to be nicknamed by her two charges, was bright, young, Scottish and with plenty of ideas of her own about how princesses should be brought up. To start with, a schoolroom was created on the floor below the nursery at 145 Piccadilly, with all the usual items such as maps and blackboards and a small desk for the Princess. A strict timetable governed school days, starting from the moment the Princess rose at 7.30. After breakfast and a quick visit to her parents there followed about four hours of lessons, interrupted by a short break for elevenses. Lunch at 1.15 was usually with her parents and the rest of the afternoon was devoted to outdoor pursuits if it was fine, otherwise to music or art. After tea at 4.45, Princess Elizabeth spent some time with the Duchess and Princess Margaret Rose in the Duchess's sitting room before supper, which was followed by bed at 7.15 for the older Princess.

Below **King George V celebrated his Silver Jubilee in 1935 and on 6 May there was a thanksgiving service in St Paul's Cathedral. The York family were first in the procession from Buckingham Palace and are here seen in Fleet Street.**

Bottom A family gathering on the balcony of Buckingham Palace after the Silver Jubilee thanksgiving service. Princess Margaret is hardly tall enough to see over the draperies.

The Yorks were doing their best to give their children a normal upbringing, as secluded as possible from the public glare, but there was no escaping their destiny. In the beginning, the public appearances were usually on family occasions. In November 1934 Princess Elizabeth was a bridesmaid for the first time when her uncle the Duke of Kent married the elegant and lovely Princess Marina of Greece in Westminster Abbey. She made her first appearance in a royal procession in May of the following year when the King celebrated the Silver Jubilee of his reign and the York family rode together in the first carriage from Buckingham Palace to St Paul's for the service of thanksgiving. The little princesses in their pink frocks and straw hats waved shyly to the crowds along the route and later in the day from the Palace balcony. A further happy event of this year was the marriage of another of the King's sons to a Scottish bride, this time the Duke of Gloucester to the Lady Alice Scott. Princess Elizabeth was becoming an accomplished bridesmaid.

Right Happy to be at home, the smiling Duchess of York leads her youngest daughter by the hand while Princess Elizabeth follows them through the grounds of Glamis Castle to see the colours being presented to the 4th and 5th Black Watch Regiment by the Duke on 10 August 1935.

Below This photograph with her father was taken in the grounds of Royal Lodge, Windsor, to celebrate the Princess's tenth birthday on 21 April 1936. An early-morning ride was a regular feature of the days at Windsor, training which would stand her in good stead for the Trooping the Colour ceremonies in the years to come.

Right The Princesses were frequent travellers, though Princess Margaret's little legs look as if they are having difficulty in keeping up with the rest of the family on this occasion.

Below Corgis have minds of their own and royal ones are no exception. Princess Elizabeth seems to be having trouble with this canine friend after one of the family's long rail journeys. With air travel still in its infancy, the royal train provided the quickest and most convenient way of getting from London to the family homes in Scotland.

One son, alas, remained unmarried, and one particular relationship of his was beginning to cause the King some concern. As George V's health deteriorated and the relationship appeared to strengthen, the concern became more universally widespread. Such worries may have exacerbated the King's decline. He was already a very sick man by the time he delivered his last Christmas broadcast, in which he passed on to the children of the Empire the greetings of his own two grand-daughters. Before the first month of the new year was up he was dead and the country had a new king.

Exceedingly popular though the Prince of Wales had been with the common people, there was a strong feeling that his proposed marriage to the twice-divorced American Mrs Simpson was something which could not be tolerated. The story of the Abdication crisis is well known, though the agonies suffered by the new King's younger brother Bertie and his wife can only be guessed at. There was certainly some debate in the popular press about whether the crown might not pass to the Duke of Kent, constitutionally a perfectly acceptable arrangement. He was a more confident and outgoing member of the family and had a son who could be groomed to succeed, thus lifting the awful burden from young female shoulders. But however self-effacing and modest he was, Prince Albert could not shirk what he felt was his duty, and so it was that Princess Elizabeth at the tender age of ten suddenly found herself daughter of a King and Heiress Presumptive.

Right Princess Elizabeth enthusiastically points out to a young friend one of the interesting goings-on down below. They are watching the 1936 Trooping the Colour ceremony from the balcony of Buckingham Palace.

Below right Leaving the 1936 Royal Tournament with their parents, the little Princesses seem somewhat dwarfed by the guard of honour. Though she can hardly have suspected it, in little over a month's time Princess Elizabeth was to become Heiress Presumptive and her father King.

Below left The newspaper headline that says it all. Having succeeded to the Throne on 20 January 1936, Edward VIII had been king for less than eleven months when he abdicated to marry the American divorcée Mrs Wallis Simpson. The Instrument of Abdication was signed at Fort Belvedere, the King's country retreat near Windsor, on 10 December.

Daily Mirror

THE DAILY MIRROR, Thursday, December 10, 1936.

No. 10305 — ONE PENNY — LONDON ED.

THE KING DECIDES: ABDICATION PLANS

DRAMATIC VISIT TO QUEEN MARY

THE KING HAS DECIDED.

His abdication—unless he makes an eleventh hour change in his decision—is regarded by the Cabinet as imminent.

His Majesty's decision will be announced by Mr. Baldwin in the House of Commons this afternoon. Lord Halifax will make a similar statement in the House of Lords.

Last night the Labour and Liberal Opposition leaders were informed by the Government of the latest moves in the crisis, and advised that there is little hope of a happy solution.

YESTERDAY AFTERNOON THE KING SLIPPED SECRETLY OUT OF FORT BELVEDERE—THE FIRST TIME HE HAD LEFT THE FORT FOR SIX DAYS—AND HE DROVE TO WINDSOR GREAT PARK, WHERE, IN ROYAL LODGE, HE HAD TEA WITH HIS MOTHER, QUEEN MARY.

This meeting was of the most moving character and had been arranged with the utmost privacy.

Elaborate precautions were taken to enable King Edward to leave the Fort unobserved.

Over Rough-Track Roads

To avoid being seen, the King left by one of the rough track roads seldom used by cars and was able to make the two-mile journey without being seen.

His car had only to traverse 200 yards of public roadway before it crossed from his estate into the long private drive through Windsor Great Park to the Lodge.

No one working in the grounds was allowed to see the King leave the house. Workmen were told to remain hidden in a garage.

After spending half an hour with his mother the King returned as secretly to the Fort.

Queen Mary was accompanied by the Princess Royal and the Earl of Athlone. Later she dined with the Duke and Duchess of Kent.

In Mr. Baldwin's private room at the House of Commons last night a special Cabinet meeting was called and Ministers were frankly told of all developments.

The King had a further consultation with his brothers, the Duke of York and the Duke of Kent at Fort Belvedere during the day. The Duke of York did not return to London till 9 p.m. He looked pale and worn. In the event of abdication he will automatically succeed to the Crown.

Throughout the day dispatch riders with important messages from London had arrived at the Fort. The King's car drove out at 8.30 and shortly before eleven o'clock the royal shooting brake which has been used for the transportation of luggage left Fort Belvedere, and also a dispatch rider.

The Duke of Kent drove to Marlborough House shortly after 8 o'clock and at 10.15 a large car entered the gates with the Duke of York as its only passenger.

M.P.s warned to be at the House to-day; Mrs. Simpson's drive.—Page 3.

KING EDWARD VIII

DIARY OF THE DAY'S EVENTS

Noon.—Mr. Walter Monckton, K.C., Attorney-General to the Duchy of Cornwall, and Sir E. Peacock back at No. 10.

1.15 p.m.—Cabinet meeting ended.

2.22 p.m.—Mr. Baldwin made his statement in Commons.

4.5 p.m.—Duke of York arrived at Fort Belvedere.

5.5 p.m.—Queen Mary meets the King at Royal Lodge, Windsor Great Park.

9.0 p.m.—Duke of York arrives back at 145.

Piccadilly. The Prime Minister, Sir John Simon and Mr. Monckton at No. 10. Succession of messengers with brief cases.

9.15 p.m.—Mr. Malcolm MacDonald at No. 10.

10.0 p.m.—Sir John Simon and Mr. Monckton again at No. 10.

10.30 p.m.—Mr. Ramsay MacDonald at Colonial Office.

11.20 p.m.—Mr. Monckton left No. 10 in the King's car.

DAUGHTER TO A KING

Opposite **A charming studio portrait of the new Queen with her young daughters, taken in 1937. Although separated in age by four years and very different in temperament, the two sisters were always devoted to each other and the nation was delighted to have such an obviously happy and close family at its head after the traumas of Edward VIII's short reign.**

Below **Young Margaret seems to be having some difficulty adjusting to the solemnity of the occasion as the Princesses watch their father's Coronation from a gallery beside Westminster Abbey's High Altar. Queen Mary and their aunt, the Princess Royal, are there to keep an eye on them.**

Princess Elizabeth and her sister were excitedly looking forward to the Coronation of their uncle when news of the Abdication filtered through to their young ears. The full import of the event was perhaps lost on them at first. It meant irritating readjustments, like having to leave the home in Piccadilly they had grown to love for the forbidding corridors of Buckingham Palace, and the clothes they had recently been measured for were now to be altered and become even grander for wear at their own father's Coronation. Princess Elizabeth probably realised more than any of her comments indicated, for she was already an astute, sensitive and self-sufficient little girl who kept her own counsel.

It seemed that there must be a change in the relationship with their father from now on, for the little Princesses were instructed to greet him with curtseys – previously reserved for their grandparents – when he returned to Piccadilly from the Accession Council which had made him King. This proved more than the King could bear, however, and it was the first and last occasion, except for formal ones, that these obeisances were practised. Queen Mary was by now resident at Marlborough House in the Mall, and it was from a window in this great mansion that she explained to her young grand-daughters the scene at St James's Palace on 12 December 1936 as the heralds proclaimed the father of the little Princesses King George VI. Much attention was henceforward to be focussed on the family, and crowds gathered outside their Piccadilly home for a glimpse of the new King and his Heiress Presumptive – 'Presumptive' and not 'Apparent' because she might yet have a brother, whose claim to the throne would take precedence over hers.

It was not till the following February that the family moved into Buckingham Palace, that vast mansion which since Queen Victoria's time has been the sovereign's principal home. Meanwhile there was a brief respite from the burden of new responsibilities in the festive celebrations at Sandringham. The enjoyment was multiplied when news came through on Christmas Day itself that a baby Princess, to be named Alexandra, had been born to the Duchess of Kent.

The new Queen did her best to create a homely atmosphere for her family at the Palace, even as outside in the Mall the peace was soon broken by the sound of workmen busy erecting stands for the crowds who would flock to the Coronation. The great day itself dawned wet, but little could dampen the enthusiasm of the two Princesses, entrusted to the care of the Princess Royal. One either side of her, they walked to their places next to Queen Mary by the High Altar to watch their father crowned. In their gowns of white and silver lace with long ermine-lined purple trains, they looked enchanting as they donned their golden coronets at the very moment their mother received her crown from the Archbishop of Canterbury. Even after the ceremony was over there were still the balcony appearances to be made and nearly an hour of official photography to be patiently endured. For her parents, Princess Elizabeth was to make her own record of the day's events, inscribed in red ink on the pages of a humble exercise book.

It was now obvious that Miss Crawford, still in her twenties, was not just educating a princess, but one destined to be queen. Most newspaper leader writers of the time agreed that Elizabeth's self-possessed but unspoilt nature was a tribute to a training being carried out on exactly the right lines. The schoolroom now overlooked the gardens of Buckingham Palace and there the Princess persevered with Bible studies, French, Latin, German, arithmetic, geometry, geography, history and English literature. She had no aptitude for mathematics, but showed above average skills in her music, dancing and drawing lessons.

Far left Eleven-year-old Elizabeth and six-year-old Margaret pose with their parents for an official photograph after the Coronation of King George VI on 12 May 1937. The setting is the Throne Room at Buckingham Palace, and the Princesses are wearing ermine-lined purple trains over gowns of white and silver lace. Their golden coronets, specially made for the occasion, are decorated with crosses and fleurs-de-lis.

Left The two Princesses seem fascinated by the exotic costumes of some of the visitors to Windsor Great Park on 19 June 1937. They were there to see King George plant the first of a Coronation grove of eighty oak trees representing all parts of the Empire.

Below, left Princess Margaret has not yet acquired her mother's elegance of posture but the family seem happy enough to be back in Scotland. They were at the Palace of Holyroodhouse in Edinburgh in July 1937 for an Inspection of the Royal Company of Archers, the Sovereign's ceremonial bodyguard when north of the Border.

Below, right Two days after the Coronation troops from the Empire were assembled in the grounds of Buckingham Palace to be presented with medals by the King.

Below Not a skill that the future Queen will ever need but Princess Elizabeth is nevertheless fascinated by the spinning ability of Mrs Mary MacLeod. Seated outside a reconstructed Highland croft, she was one of the exhibits at the 1938 Empire Exhibition held in Glasgow, at which Princess Elizabeth was the ten millionth visitor.

Right Riding remained a great pleasure for the King and his daughters even after his brother's abdication had cast an enormous extra burden of work on to his shoulders. The Princesses' buttonholes on this occasion are probably in celebration of Elizabeth's twelfth birthday on 21 April 1938.

Left A blissful summer day for Princesses and pet. The gardens of Royal Lodge in the south-east corner of Windsor Great Park provided a delightful retreat far from the public gaze for two little girls who liked nothing better than to play with their corgis and Labradors.

Right Highlight of a visit to London Zoo on 30 June 1938 was an inspection of the Penguin Pool. One of its inhabitants does not seem too keen on shaking flippers with Princess Elizabeth's companion. The two royal children were to make several visits to the zoo while their parents were away in Canada and the United States and obviously enjoyed every minute.

Queen Mary began to take a closer interest in her granddaughter's education and whisked her off on visits to Kensington Palace (where both she herself and Queen Victoria had been born), the National Portrait Gallery and various museums. On the advice of Kenneth Clark, then surveyor of the royal pictures, items from the magnificent royal collection were borrowed for week-long display in the schoolroom, where at the age of seven Princess Margaret was brought in to join her sister.

All was not unrelieved happiness at this time. In 1938, shortly before the King and Queen set off for a triumphant state visit to France, the Princesses' loved maternal grandmother, Lady Strathmore, died. Elizabeth's sympathy went out wholeheartedly to her mother, whose sorrow must at such cost be hidden from public view. The following year a much longer visit was planned, this time to Canada and the United States. President Roosevelt longed to entertain the two Princesses but their father decided they were far too young for such a gruelling trip. Instead they went down by train with Queen Mary to Portsmouth to wave goodby as *The Empress of Australia* set sail for the New World. The seven weeks of parental absence were enlivened by one of Miss Crawford's novel excursions, this time on a London Underground train, from which they emerged, not altogether unnoticed, at Tottenham Court Road station to take tea at the YWCA.

Opposite, top A famous first meeting. This may not have been the first time Princess Elizabeth and Prince Philip (left) actually met, but it was the first occasion on which they were photographed together. Elizabeth was just thirteen and visiting Dartmouth College with her parents and sister in June 1939. The young naval cadet chosen to show them round was Lord Mountbatten's nephew, with whom the future Queen was soon to start up a long correspondence leading eventually to courtship and marriage.

Opposite, bottom When the King and Queen returned from their triumphant visit to Canada and the United States on 22 June 1939 the two Princesses were reunited with them on the *Empress of Britain* in the Solent. While on board they were presented with these two giant pandas by the crew.

Below Looking at a map of Canada in anticipation of the King and Queen's 1939 tour.

Above **Queen Mary** was fond of taking her grand-daughters on educational visits; in May 1939 the three of them toured the London docks aboard the steamer *St Katherine*. Other favourite venues were the National Portrait Gallery and Kensington Palace, scene of the Queen's birth on 26 May 1867.

Right A nostalgic occasion, even for royal youngsters. Princess Margaret, nursing a doll, stands by the cot in which she used to sleep at 145 Piccadilly. The house was opened up to the public in July 1939 for an Exhibition of Royal Treasures which the Princesses were among the first to attend.

Opposite, bottom More Royal Treasures at 145 Piccadilly. Did the Princesses remember any of these items from their early childhood? The house where they had been so happy was to be destoryed by air raids in 1941.

Below The war saw to it that there were not too many treats for the Princesses when they were growing up, but the Queen, herself a keen theatre-goer, was anxious that they should not miss out entirely on the pleasure to be derived from live performances. It was perhaps Princess Margaret who inherited her mother's enthusiasm most completely.

June, the month of their parents' return, also saw the now famous visit to the Royal Naval College at Dartmouth during which Princess Elizabeth's affections are said to have first been engaged by a dashing young naval cadet four years her senior who was acting as royal guide. She and Prince Philip had probably met many times previously since the Prince was nephew to Lord Louis Mountbatten, a close friend of the family. But on this occasion the Princess's eyes seldom left him and it was not long afterwards that a correspondence started up between the future queen and the young midshipman just starting out on his naval career.

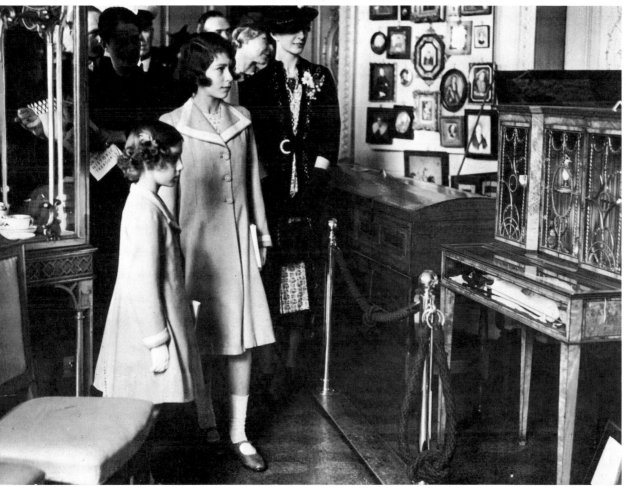

Above **Springtime in Windsor Great Park, 1940. The Queen has always loved flowers and even today likes to work surrounded by them. She has probably received more bouquets than any other woman alive but still appreciates the simple pleasure to be derived from less exotic blooms such as the daffodil.**

Opposite **Determined to do her bit towards the war effort, Princess Elizabeth broadcast to the children of the Empire on 13 October 1940 with her sister sitting beside her watching the microphones with fascination. She had been coached beforehand by her mother and in the event performed faultlessly.**

Elizabeth was thirteen-and-a-half when war was declared against Germany on 3 September 1939 and she heard her father and the Prime Minister Neville Chamberlain address the people on the wireless. At the time she was resident at Balmoral and it was decided that for their own safety she and her sister should be kept out of London during hostilities. Thus it was that she spent the next few months at Birkhall, the secluded Jacobean house by the River Muick on the Balmoral estate, surrounded by evacuees from Glasgow and helping out with Red Cross sewing parties. This exile from her parents was short-lived, however, and by January 1940 she was back at Royal Lodge, Windsor, from which she moved in May to the greater safety of Windsor Castle, her home for most of the war. It was gloomier than usual, for many of the furnishings had been dismantled and stored away for better protection, and the Princesses were to be ushered to the safety of the dungeons at the first sign of an air-raid.

Many voices urged that the Princesses should not be in Britain at all. In the summer of 1940 the French had surrendered and Hitler was declaring that his troops would be marching through London on 15 September. The King was torn between the desirability of having the heiress out of harm's way and the need to sustain public confidence. The Queen's views also had to be considered: 'The Princesses cannot go without me. I cannot go without the King. The King will never go.' And so they stayed.

Princess Elizabeth was desperate to make as great a contribution to the war effort as it was in her power to do, and it was at her own suggestion that on 13 October 1940 she broadcast to the children of the Empire. She rehearsed her delivery over and over again with her mother and performed faultlessly when the time came, sounding to the King's ear uncannily like his wife. The message was one of cheerfulness and courage at home and support for the troops abroad, in the certainty that all in the end would be well. So that her sister, continually in her shadow, should not feel left out, she called on her to join in the final 'Good night, children'. Listening in her wartime refuge at Badminton House the old Queen Mother was moved to tears by the simple sincerity in her grand-daughter's voice.

In spite of the war's upheavals the Princess's education had to go on. It was a lucky chance that Windsor was so close to Eton, for it meant that the Vice-Provost Henry Marten, distinguished author and historian, could help to educate the future queen in those intricacies of Constitutional History which were beyond the skills of Miss Crawford to describe. Elizabeth was fourteen when she started her hour-a-week sessions learning about the powers of Crown, Parliament, Church and the Law. As she got older the lessons became twice-weekly and to the courses of study were added history lessons on the colonies and the dominions and lectures on national expenditure. Systematic reading of the national news-papers provided the basis for discussions about current affairs and political leaders. As parts of Windsor Great Park went under the plough in the cause of increased home food production even this event was used educationally – to spark off an investigation into the evolution of English agriculture. For few others can learning have had such immediate relevance.

Above **The Royal Chapel of All Saints, the little church close to the Royal Lodge in the private area of Windsor Great Park where the Royal Family usually worship when at Windsor. They have their own pew in the chancel out of sight of the rest of the congregation, mainly other residents on the Windsor estates.**

Opposite, top **The King and his elder daughter in the quiet of his study at Windsor in 1942. He was gradually educating Princess Elizabeth in the tasks that would one day be hers and introducing her to the red dispatch boxes containing Foreign Office documents which have to be dealt with by the monarch nearly every day.**

Opposite, bottom **A relaxed moment on the lawn at Windsor Castle with the Princesses' corgi Jane. In the background is the imposing East Front of the Castle behind which are the Private Apartments of the Royal Family. This is one of a delightful series of photographs taken at Windsor in 1941.**

In the Trench during an alert for flying bombs. Anne Crichton Ruth Melden, Dawn Simpson, Greina & Muriel Murray Brown, Pat Hobbs, Josephine Burwell Smith, Self, and Iris Woods. Camp at Frogmore July 1944

Left A photograph from the Princess's personal collection, annotated in her hand. Sea Rangers camping at Frogmore in July 1944 had to take refuge in this trench when there was a flying-bomb alert. The Princess is second from the bottom, enjoying the novel experience as much as her friends.

Opposite The education of the Princesses, and in particular the Heir to the Throne, had to continue in spite of the war. Here the Queen supervises her daughters' studies in the grounds of Windsor Castle in July 1941. Princess Elizabeth was fourteen when she started her weekly lessons with Henry Marten, Vice-Provost of nearby Eton College.

As the war went on the Princess longed to be in uniform. For the moment the only one she was entitled to was that of a Girl Guide. Back in 1938 in response to the Princess's pleadings a company had been formed at the Palace, its members drawn from the children of staff there and cousins and friends brought in from outside. Too young to be a Guide, Princess Margaret had been enrolled as a Brownie and the pair of them had made their first official appearance in uniform in June 1938 at a Girl Guide Review carried out by the King and Queen at Windsor. Early on in the war a Girl Guide company had been started up at Windsor with Elizabeth as a Patrol Leader, though she was shortly to graduate to the Sea Rangers, learning to sail on the lake at Frogmore and earning her bosun's badge and several proficiency awards. The grounds at Windsor allowed many other activities to be pursued and there were gardening expeditions to Royal Lodge which had been opened up again to allow the King a place for relaxation 'away from it all' in the home he had helped to create.

Pages 46–47 Royal Lodge, Windsor Great Park. In 1931 it was given by George V to the Yorks who immediately set about transforming the gardens and making the house such a comfortable place that it has been a royal favourite ever since. Princess Elizabeth spent the first months of 1940 here but then had to move to the safety of the castle.

Page 47, inset The Octagon Room at Royal Lodge, Windsor. From its windows there are lovely views over the gardens. Although not considered a safe refuge in the early years of the war, the house was opened up again later on and the Royal Family were able to enjoy many happy hours here, particularly in the gardens which were the delight of the King.

Sadly, that scene of so much childhood enjoyment, 145 Piccadilly, was gutted by air raids in 1941. Before the war it had been opened up to become such a tourist attraction that its continued existence was perhaps an embarrassment for the family. The Princesses were made even more directly aware of the tragedies of war when the Palace itself was bombed, an event to be repeated another eight times. Perhaps the saddest moment of all came in August 1942 when the King was called from the dinner table at Balmoral to be told that his brother George's plane had crashed into a Scottish mountainside killing him instantaneously.

In the darkest days the whole family derived great comfort from their religious faith, and witness to this faith was given by the Princess's confirmation on 1 March 1942, shortly before her sixteenth birthday. The day before, Dr Cosmo Lang, the Archbishop of Canterbury who had officiated at her parents' wedding and crowned her father, journeyed down to Windsor to offer his spiritual counsel to the future Supreme Governor of the Church of England. The confirmation itself was carried out by the Canon of St George's Chapel at a quiet private ceremony in the Castle.

Opposite, top The Royal Family pose for wartime cameras at Buckingham Palace in 1942. The King and Queen hoped to boost morale by staying in London and sharing the hardships of their subjects in the capital. In fact the Palace was to be bombed nine times altogether.

Below Looking at this idyllic scene photographed at Windsor in 1941 it is difficult to imagine that it was wartime. Many had called for the Princesses to be evacuated to somewhere safe like Canada as many of their contemporaries had been but the Queen insisted on staying by the side of the King and having her daughters with her.

Below Princess Elizabeth (sitting extreme left) adds her cheerful presence to this happy family group, taken to mark the christening of Prince Michael in 1942. Sadly it was the last for which his father, the Duke of Kent (standing centre), posed. Less than two months after his son's birth he was killed when his plane crashed into a Scottish mountainside.

If Elizabeth's deep religious faith was inherited from her parents, so too was her love of music. From their nursery days it had been the Duchess's habit to play the piano to her children, and later the family had developed the custom of gathering round for a singsong. Anything from old Scottish songs and English ballads to Negro spirituals might be heard emanating from whatever room the piano was in. The Princess followed her mother's example, starting piano lessons at the age of four and eventually learning to play both the great classics and the popular dance music of the day.

Above The two Princesses at Buckingham Palace in May 1942. For their own safety they spent most of the war at Windsor Castle where they could be ushered to the safety of the dungeons at the first sound of an air raid.

Above, right The Princesses were only too well aware of the need for them to set an example. Here they are seen helping the war effort by buying War Savings Certificates at a country Post Office in January 1943.

Below The Princess became Colonel of the Grenadier Guards when she was only fifteen. In April 1943 she paid a visit to an armoured battalion of the Grenadiers in Southern Command and is here seen greeting officers and Eton cadets attached to the battalion for training.

Opposite A charming portrait of the seventeen-year-old heir to the throne, taken by world-famous photographer, Karsh of Ottawa. By 1943 she was really beginning to look like a young woman rather than a schoolgirl, and shows a great deal of naturalness in front of the camera.

The Queen was anxious that this interest in music should be developed; accordingly the organist of St George's Chapel, Dr Harris, was asked to talk to the two Princesses about the great composers and their masterpieces. Every Tuesday they visited his house in the Castle Cloisters for this purpose and there were trips up into the organ loft of St George's to hear him play. The Chapel choristers were roped in for a series of musical parties at which the Princesses, with their clear soprano voices, were joined by their friends for the singing of part-songs and madrigals under the direction of Dr Harris. Soon his house became too small for the events and they were moved to the Red Drawing Room at the Castle, where the Queen provided an occasional audience of one.

Above **Sandringham House in Norfolk was a favourite home of the King, and the Royal Family were able to visit it during the war. Much of the estate was under cultivation as part of the war effort and the Queen is here seen inspecting the 1943 harvest from the comfort of her pony trap while her husband and daughters take to their bicycles.**

Opposite, top **Some of the happiest moments of the war years were provided by the pantomimes held annually at Windsor. This is the 1944 production of** *Old Mother Red Riding Boots,* **a medley of pantomimes. Princess Elizabeth in a lacy pink dress of the 1890s is admiring the haul of shrimps brought in by her sister and a sailor friend from the sea at Brighton.**

Opposite, bottom **The year 1944 was a very significant one for the Princess for it saw her coming of age. This family group was gathered together to celebrate her eighteenth birthday on 21 April 1944. The King, as so often during the war, is wearing his Army uniform.**

Another natural talent to be developed was acting and the Queen again took the initiative by asking Hubert Tannar, Headmaster of the Royal School at Windsor, if the Princesses could join his pupils in a concert to be given at the school. So successful was it, with the Princesses playing the piano as well as acting in a scene specially written by Mr Tannar, that the Queen ordered a 'Command Performance' at the Castle. What started as a 'one-off' event developed into a tradition and every Christmas during the following war years a show was given. In 1940 Princess Elizabeth, wearing a make-believe crown, was playing one of the Three Kings in a nativity play; thereafter it was pantomimes, usually with Elizabeth as principal boy opposite her sister's leading lady. Prince Philip was reportedly in the front row of the audience at the 1943 production of *Aladdin.* A year later the King was delighted to find his elder daughter playing a woman for once, enchantingly dressed in the height of Edwardian fashion for her role in a medley of pantomimes called *Old Mother Red Riding Boots.*

The year 1944 was a momentous one for Princess Elizabeth for it was the year she celebrated her eighteenth birthday and started to undertake public engagements in earnest. King George was increasingly confident of his daughter's knowledge and under-standing of current affairs, which were being broadened by her involvement in his working sessions with the boxes of state papers delivered almost daily. He was therefore somewhat astonished to discover that if anything should happen to him – and he was of course a prime target for the enemy – Elizabeth would be required to rule under a regent until she attained the age of twenty-one. This factor became particularly relevant when the King decided to visit the forces in North Africa in July 1944; he discovered that, because of her age, his daughter could not become a Counsellor of State, one of those appointed to exercise the royal functions in his absence. It needed an amendment of the Regency Act to alter this anomaly and an amendment there duly was, carried the more easily no doubt because others shared the King's high estimation of his daughter.

Until she was eighteen the Princess had had no special apartments of her own at the Palace in which to receive official visitors. So much in demand were her services becoming that it was felt this situation must be remedied and thus she came to inherit the Princess Royal's former sitting-room. She also needed a 'Household' to help her cope with the increasing workload, and on 11 July 1944 she was given her first lady-in-waiting, Lady Mary Strachey, who was to accompany her on public appearances and help deal with the large postbag. So great was the burden becoming that in March of the following year another lady-in-waiting, Mrs Vicary Gibbs, arrived to ease matters, to be joined by a third in May, Lady Margaret Egerton. They were all young women in their mid-twenties, old enough to have some confidence and experience of the world but of an age to provide the Princess with companionship in what was otherwise a most lonely position.

Opposite, top **In June 1945 Princess Elizabeth undertook her first solo engagement in Wales when she had the daunting task of addressing over 4,000 people at a Girl Guide council meeting in Cardiff. The royal limousine had an opening roof which enabled the Princess to stand up in it and be seen more easily by the huge crowds who came out to greet her.**

Below **The King donned his Air Force uniform for this visit to Bomber Command with his wife and elder daughter in July 1944. The men posing with them had just returned from an attack on flying-bomb installations in France.**

Above **Their Colonel inspects the Grenadier Guards at their Wellington Barracks on 7 May 1945. The Princess was by now entitled to wear a uniform herself, that of an ATS subaltern, though the war was virtually over.**

One of Elizabeth's first appointments had been as Colonel of the Grenadier Guards and she had early experience of inspecting a tank battalion on her own and taking the salute at a march-past. Service appointments were to figure large in the future, but to begin with she concentrated her efforts on other causes close to her heart and in particular the well-being of the young. With this in mind her first official visit on her own to the City of London, on 31 May 1944, was to be installed at the Mansion House as President of the National Society for the Prevention of Cruelty to Children. Scotland's turn came on 23 September when she was present in Edinburgh's Assembly Hall to receive on behalf of the YMCA money collected for its appeal fund. It was not until 2 June 1945 that she was in Cardiff, attending a council meeting of Girl Guides where she had the daunting task of addressing over four thousand people.

58

The Princess's first major social appearance, in effect perhaps her 'coming out', was at a big official dinner party on 1 May 1944 when she found herself sandwiched between the two elder statesmen of the Commonwealth, Field Marshal Smuts, Prime Minister of South Africa, and Mr Mackenzie King, Prime Minister of Canada, at a Buckingham Palace function given in their honour. It was a useful foretaste of things to come and apparently the Princess made a very good listener, intent to glean some of the wisdom accumulated by their years.

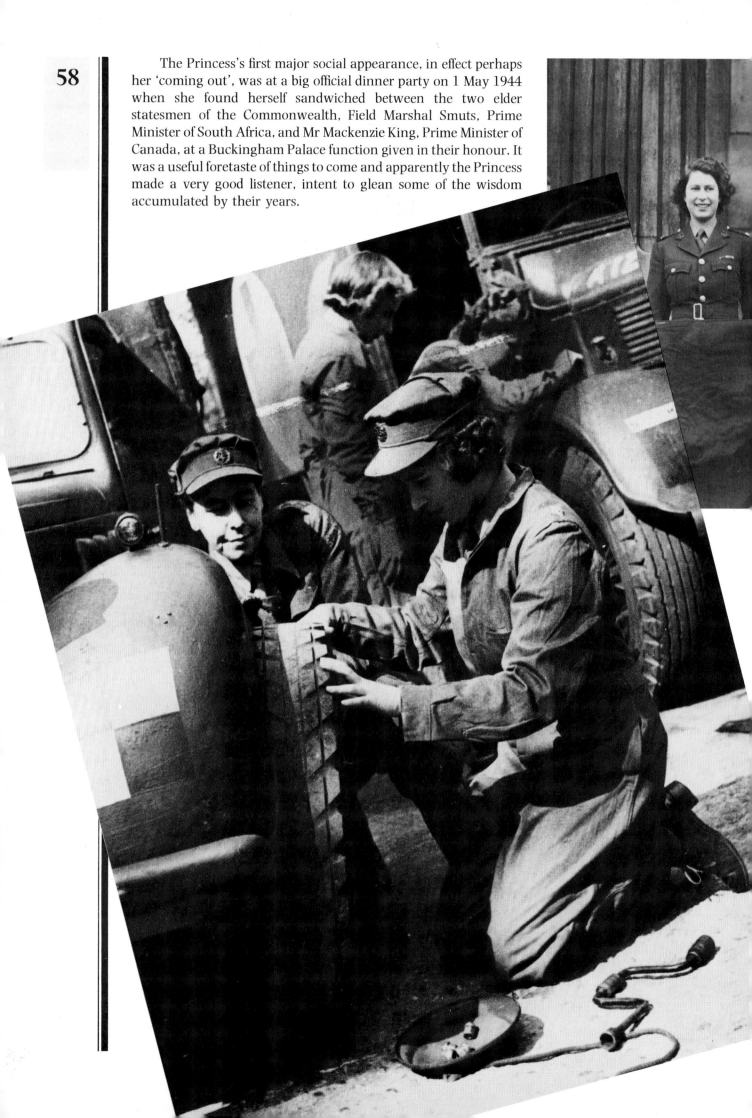

Above **Princess Elizabeth was proudly wearing her ATS uniform on VE-Day, 8 May 1945. In an unprecedented gesture Winston Churchill, the hero of the hour, was invited to join the Royal Family on the balcony of Buckingham Palace to acknowledge the thanks of a grateful people.**

Opposite **Second Subaltern No. 230873 Windsor tries her hand at changing the wheel of an ambulance under the watchful eye of her instructor. She started her ATS career in March 1945 at No. 1 Mechanical Transport Training Centre, Aldershot, and emerged with flying colours.**

For security reasons some of her engagements had to be kept secret. There was no advance public notification that she would be at John Brown's Clydebank shipyard on 30 November 1944 to launch the battleship *Vanguard*. Mercifully, because of the German collapse, it was not to fire its guns in anger; instead one of its first missions would be to carry the Royal Family to South Africa for the state visit of 1947.

Although she was certainly doing her bit to boost public morale, the Princess continued to feel frustrated that her privileged position seemed to be protecting her from the claims of ordinary national service. Eventually the King gave in to her pleadings and she was allowed to join the ATS. So it was that Second Subaltern No. 230873 Windsor arrived in March 1945 at No. 1 Mechanical Transport Training Centre, Aldershot, to begin the NCO's course in the theory and practice of mechanics. She, who had never so much as driven a car, within weeks was venturing on to the road in a 15cwt Bedford lorry. She learnt to drive two other types of vehicle too – a Wolseley staff car and a large field ambulance – as well as mastering other ATS essentials such as map-reading, night-driving and first aid.

No publicity was given to the Princess's whereabouts and, apart from the fact that she was allowed home to Windsor every night, she was treated like any other junior officer. It was therefore with blackened hands and in greasy overalls that she greeted the rest of her family when they went down to see how she was getting on. In fact she was found underneath a car which she would have succeeded in getting started had not the King secretly unclipped the distributor cap. This proved but a temporary setback in her army career and by the time she finished her course the Princess had done well enough to be pronounced 'a very good and extremely considerate driver' by her company commander.

Left A charming smile from the Princess for the people of Lewisham during the Royal Family's Victory Tour of South London on 10 May. Her parents had made a point of visiting bomb-stricken parts of the capital during the war and must have been delighted that there was now a chance to share joy as well as sorrow.

Below On 13 May 1945, the first Sunday after VE-Day, there was a Service of Thanksgiving at St Paul's Cathedral attended by the Royal Family. The nineteen-year-old Princess Elizabeth, though relieved like everyone else to see the end of the war in Europe, must still have been worrying about the safety of Prince Philip whose war was not to end until he witnessed the Japanese surrender in Tokyo Bay on 2 September.

Having truly earnt her right to it, the Princess wore her uniform of ATS Junior Commander on many occasions and with pride. She was wearing it on the balcony of Buckingham Palace on the evening of VE-Day where, in an unprecedented gesture of tribute to the inspirational leadership he had provided during the war, Winston Churchill was invited to join the Royal Family. Eight times they were called out to acknowledge the cheers of a people grateful for victory and for the noble and courageous example set them by the highest in the land. On such an exceptional day the Princesses were allowed to slip out of the Palace with some officers of the Brigade of Guards to join in the celebrations down below, truly at one with the people in their hour of greatest rejoicing, but to all appearances just two ordinary high-spirited teenage girls.

Princess Elizabeth was with her parents on the victory tours of the capital which followed, driving with them through streets full of cheering Londoners, and again on VJ-Day, but this time she made her balcony appearance in civilian clothes. Even in the midst of victory no one could forget at what cost the war had been won, especially in terms of human lives. At the Service of Remembrance at the Cenotaph in Whitehall that year Princess Elizabeth herself came forward to lay a wreath on behalf of those of her own age, many of whom had perished in the holocaust. She had taken part with them in the great struggle against evil and was acknowledging the sacrifice which had helped to mould the world she and her generation now inherited.

WIFE AND MOTHER

Princess Anne was a daredevil even before she could walk. Here she sets off to explore the garden at Clarence House. In only a year's time these carefree days would be a thing of the past as King George's death cast the burden of queenship on to the mother's young shoulders.

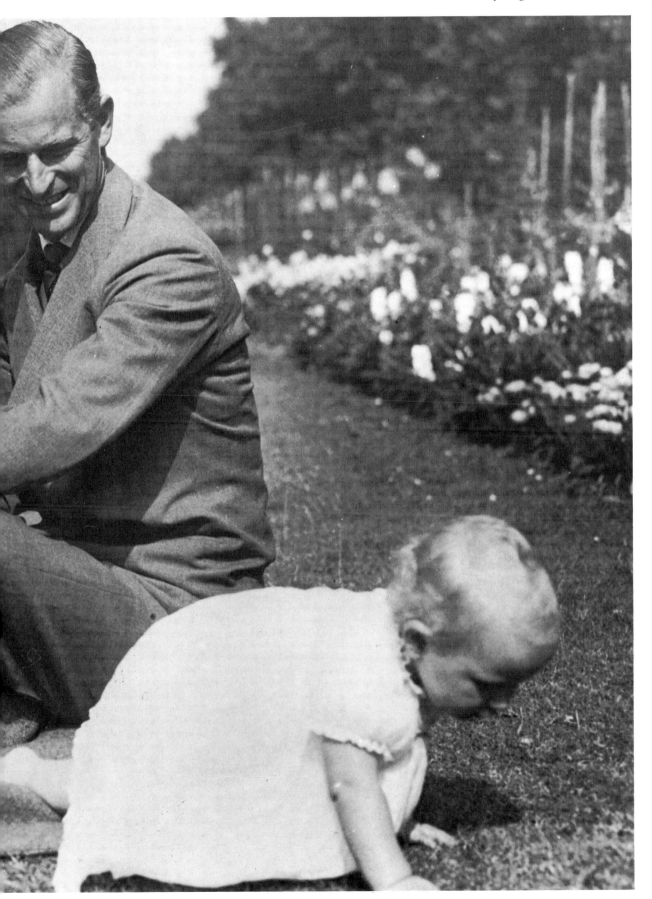

It was extremely fortunate, in view of the sad experiences of her uncle and her sister, that the instincts of her heart led Princess Elizabeth in the direction of one so eminently fitted for the role of Queen's consort. The young man, for whose safety she must have prayed throughout those seemingly endless war years, was not only a Prince in his own right, but one of qualities already proven in the service of his adopted country.

Although a Prince of Greece, Philip in fact belonged to a branch of the Danish royal family which had been called in to rule the Hellenes in 1863 when that country was looking to recover its stability with the aid of a new dynasty. Prince Philip's grandfather, brother of Edward VII's Queen Alexandra, had been the first ruler of that dynasty as King George I. His father Andrew, who died in 1944, was the fourth son of the King and a commander in the Greek army during the First World War. He married Princess Alice, daughter of the great admiral Prince Louis of Battenberg, who with Winston Churchill was responsible for reorganising the Royal Navy in preparation for the 1914–18 hostilities. Prince Louis had thought it wise to renounce his German title during the war and was created an English peer, becoming the Marquess of Milford Haven. His family name of Battenberg was meanwhile translated into one destined for particular distinction – Mountbatten.

Prince Philip, younger brother to four sisters, was born on Corfu on 10 June 1921. He spent most of his earliest years in France before being sent at the age of seven to an English prep school, Cheam. It was probably the magnetic draw of its headmaster which then took him to Kurt Hahn's school in Germany, but the black clouds of Hitler's National Socialism were gathering so fast that soon school, headmaster and many pupils were moved to Gordonstoun in Aberdeenshire, Scotland. Prince Philip was one of the lucky ones and stayed on to become head of the school. A concentration on physical toughness allied to community service made for a vigorous regime which obviously served him well, for Prince Philip felt himself to have gained so much from the experience that he was to send his own sons there.

Above **A happy portrait of father and daughter in the grounds of Royal Lodge, Windsor, in July 1946.**

Opposite, top **Not born to be King, the young Prince Philip (seated) missed playing the lead in the 1935 production of** *Macbeth* **at his Scottish school, Gordonstoun, but nevertheless landed a noble part.**

Opposite, bottom **The royal sisters set to swab the decks with bucket and brooms when they visited the training vessel HMS** *Duke of York* **in July 1946.**

Below **The Victory Parade was held in London on 8 June 1946.**

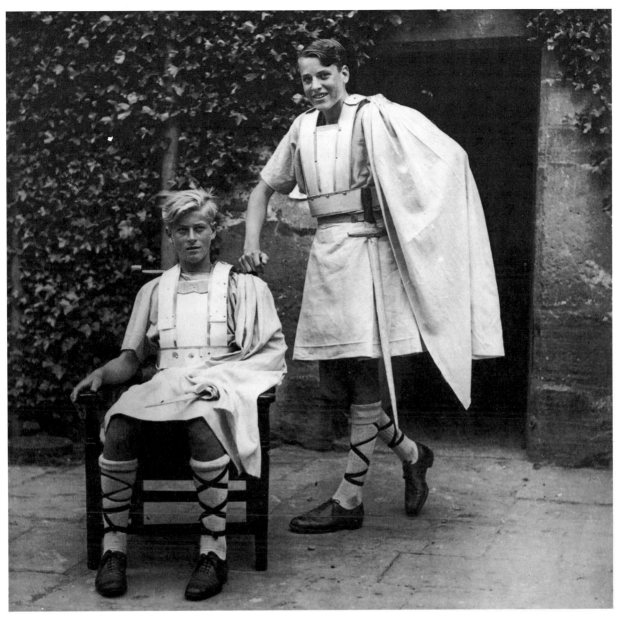

The time spent sailing small boats along the Scottish coast gave Prince Philip a love of the sea which was translated into something more positive when he entered the Navy in 1939 and emerged from the Royal Naval College as the best all-round cadet of his term. The year 1940 brought active service with the Mediterranean Fleet and before he was twenty he had been mentioned in war dispatches. A very distinguished naval career looked even more certain when he was appointed First Lieutenant of HMS *Wallace* at the exceptionally early age of twenty-one. As the war ended Prince Philip was executive officer of the destroyer HMS *Whelp* from whose deck he witnessed the surrender of the Japanese fleet in Tokyo Bay on 2 September 1945.

Princess Elizabeth must have thrilled to news of these exploits reported back in Philip's letters. She must also have breathed a sigh of relief when there was no longer a need for acts of bravery and heroism and she could hope to be reunited with the prince whose photograph had adorned her bedroom for the past two years. There was no time to daydream, however, for her official engagements became increasingly demanding. Apart from various reviews of the Armed Forces, perhaps the most interesting of her 1946 activities were the visits to Northern Ireland and to the National Eisteddfod in Glamorgan.

66

As the Princess journeyed across the Irish Sea in March on board the cruiser HMS *Superb*, she must have experienced some trepidation. The most important solo engagement of her public career so far lay ahead of her and this was the first time in her life that she had travelled beyond the British mainland. In the event she performed faultlessly, launching in Belfast HMS *Eagle*, then the largest aircraft carrier in the world, and afterwards delivering a speech at a luncheon in the city. A tour through three counties covering over two hundred miles gave many people in a somewhat neglected part of the kingdom a chance to see the young woman who would one day rule over them.

From the technologies of a new age to the mysteries of the past, as five months later the Princess ascended Mountain Ash wearing the green robe of an Ovate, to be welcomed as a new Bard by the Arch-Druid before declaring the National Eisteddfod open with a few words of Welsh specially learnt for the occasion. It was a gesture greatly appreciated by the crowd as they joined in a glorious finale to sing 'Land of my Fathers' as only the Welsh can.

Bottom **Princess Elizabeth's investiture as an Honorary Ovate of the Gorsedd of Bards on 6 August 1946.**

Opposite **In Northern Ireland to launch HMS *Eagle* in March 1946.**

Below **An 'illicit' Irish still!**

The King felt the war had deprived his daughters of much of the joy they should have had in their teenage years and although these were still the days of austerity, with food and clothes rationing, Princess Elizabeth was encouraged to discover the pleasures of theatre- and concert-going, dancing and horse-racing. This latter was a particular favourite of the King and his wife, who were delighted to discover a similar enthusiasm develop in their elder daughter from the moment she attended her first race meeting that year at Ascot.

The King was especially anxious that the Princess should meet more young men, for he was worried that this attachment so obviously forming between her and the young naval officer was a product of the narrowness of the Princess's experience. Like many a father he was loath to lose his daughter to another man so soon and worried that young love might not prove lasting. Princess Elizabeth showed herself a tireless partner to the dozens of young men from the great families of England who were seen dancing in her company and who provided the newspapers of the day with endless scope for speculation. The frequent visits of a Greek prince to Windsor seemed of little significance.

The Princess herself had very decidedly made up her mind and so had the Prince, ready to sacrifice an exceptionally promising career in the cause of love. Meanwhile an invitation had reached the King which was to prolong their agony further. By the Royal Marriage Act of 1772 the Princess could not marry without her father's consent, and he was not yet ready, in spite of her pleadings, to give that consent, insisting instead that the young couple's love should be tested by more months of separation. It was an invitation from Field Marshall Smuts for all the Royal Family to visit South Africa that provided the King with his opportunity. So it was that on a frosty February day in 1947 the 'Firm of Four', as the King liked to describe his family, sailed from Southampton on HMS *Vanguard*, the Princess's thoughts more with one left behind than with those about to greet her.

Below **Both Princesses acted as bridesmaids at the wedding of Lord Mountbatten's daughter Patricia to Lord Brabourne at Romsey Abbey on 26 October 1946. No one at the time drew any conclusions from the presence there of Lieutenant Philip Mountbatten since he was the bride's cousin.**

Right Princes Elizabeth brings a ray of sunshine to a grateful patient at the Princess Elizabeth Orthopaedic Hospital. Still only twenty, she had nevertheless thrown herself wholeheartedly into her royal duties, giving her time most generously when it could help the young and disabled.

Below In spite of the enforced separation from Prince Philip, Elizabeth is obviously managing to enjoy the deck games on HMS *Vanguard* as it makes its way to South Africa for the Royal Tour of 1947. This is one of a series of happy photographs radioed back to Britain from the ship in February.

Opposite **On 12 June 1947 Princess Elizabeth took part in the Trooping the Colour ceremony for the first time. She wore the uniform of a colonel and rode side-saddle as the King's principal supporter. Her great-great-grandmother Queen Victoria, in the early years of her reign, had been the first woman to ride in uniform at such a ceremony.**

The South African tour was in many respects the dream of any tourist of the day. Even before they arrived there was the excitement of the fun and games on board ship, in particular the 'Crossing the Line' ceremonies when crew members dressed up as Father Neptune and his entourage initiate those crossing the equator for the first time into the freedom of the seas by subjecting them to various indignities including a ducking in the ship's pool. Then a tour which included visits to an ostrich farm, a game park, diamond mines and, most wonderful of all, the Victoria Falls, could hardly have failed to excite even the most lovelorn. Although the King, first monarch ever to visit the country, was the centre of attraction, Princess Elizabeth was invited to open a dry dock named after her in East London, Cape Province and there were generous presents for both Princesses wherever they went, with diamond heaped upon diamond.

It was a significant visit for the Princess in more ways than one. Leaving aside the emotional traumas, it was the first time she had journeyed outside the British Isles; most important of all, it was in South Africa, 6,000 miles from home, that she would celebrate her coming of age. It was the occasion for a moving broadcast to all the peoples of South Africa and to others listening in the Commonwealth in which she dedicated herself with the words: 'I declare before you all that my whole life, whether it be long or short, shall be devoted to your service and the service of our great Imperial Commonwealth to which we all belong.'

There were celebratory balls and a cake for the Princess, as well as more diamonds. Another touching moment in the tour

Below **The Princess arrives at the Dorchester Hotel for the 1947 Royal and Merchant Navy Ball. The gentleman in attendance is Lord Rupert Nevill, who was to become Prince Philip's Private Secretary in 1976.**

came later and in another country, as the Princess appeared to make a barefoot pilgrimage to the grave of Cecil Rhodes on a hill just outside Bulawayo. In fact, it was a sacrificial gesture for her mother whose own shoes had proved inadequate for the ascent.

Back in the home country the King's subjects had been enduring one of the coldest winters on record, made the less bearable by the continuing coal shortages. A seemingly minor event had been Prince Philip's renunciation of his Greek title and assumption of British nationality. Now a commoner, he had adopted his mother's maiden name, Mountbatten, as a surname. Though it was not general knowledge at the time, elaborate arrangements had been made to allow this gentleman regular telephone contact with the heir to the throne whenever the White Train in which she was travelling stopped long enough for communications to be established. On 11 May, when the need for such devices was at an end, it was plain Lieutenant Mountbatten who was reunited with his bride-to-be at the Palace.

As if to make up for her previous absence, events seemed to crowd in on the Princess. There were more visits to factories and workshops to meet ordinary people doing their ordinary jobs as well as the involvement in more formal functions. On his official birthday, 12 June, the King bestowed on his eldest daughter the Imperial Order of the Crown of India and she rode as his principal supporter at the Trooping the Colour ceremony, riding side-saddle and wearing a modified version of a Life Guard's uniform with a collar and tie and the crown and stars of a colonel. A month later it was the City of London's turn to honour her with its Freedom at the Guildhall. Then, on 9 July 1947, the nation thrilled to a statement issued from the Palace: 'It is with the greatest pleasure that The King and Queen announce the betrothal of their dearly beloved daughter The Princess Elizabeth to Lieutenant Philip Mountbatten, RN, son of the late Prince Andrew of Greece and Princess Andrew (Princess Alice of Battenberg), to which union The King has gladly given his consent.' The following day there was a garden party at the Palace where the Princess could show off her future husband and the engagement ring of diamonds and platinum which had once belonged to his mother.

Royal weddings generally follow soon after royal engagements and Princess Elizabeth's was no exception, 20 November being the day fixed upon. There was much speculation about what kind of wedding it would be in view of the post-war austerity. But it is seldom that an heiress to the throne marries and to the King it seemed an occasion which might lift tired spirits with new hope in the future. Accordingly Westminster Abbey was designated as the setting and with her mother's advice the Princess chose one of the more elaborate and glamorous of the creations submitted to her by dressmaker Norman Hartnell and was allowed some extra clothes coupons for it. The design was a secret revealed only on the day itself as the twenty-one-year-old Princess emerged with her father from Buckingham Palace in the Irish State Coach guarded by the Sovereign's Escort of Life Guards and Blues.

Everything was splendid for the occasion, the Household Cavalry in uniforms not worn since 1939, the clergy officiating at the Abbey in their embroidered copes, the Gentlemen-at-Arms resplendent in scarlet uniforms and plumed helmets. To carry the bride's long train, there were her young cousins Princes William of Gloucester and Michael of Kent, handsomely fitted out in kilts of Royal Stewart tartan, and there were no less than eight

Above **The newly engaged couple at Buckingham Palace.**

Opposite **One of the happiest days of Princess Elizabeth's life was undoubtedly 9 July 1947. After a long courtship and more than three months' separation the engagement of the King's eldest daughter to Lieutenant Philip Mountbatten, RN, was at last announced to the world. With his future bride and in-laws Philip poses for the photographer in the White Drawing Room of Buckingham Palace.**

bridesmaids, among them Princess Margaret and Princess Alexandra, all dressed in embroidered white tulle which complemented beautifully the pure white silk of the bride's gown. Woven in Dundee, it had been embroidered in flower patterns with hundreds of tiny seed pearls by the patient Hartnell seamstresses. They were rewarded with their own seats in the Abbey, mingling with kings, queens, Commonwealth statesmen, cabinet ministers and countless relatives and friends of bride and groom.

Waiting for the Princess at the altar, as her father led her through the Great West Door of the Abbey, was the man who that morning had been given the style 'His Royal Highness' and been created Duke of Edinburgh, Earl of Merionith and Baron Greenwich. The naval associations were hardly to be forgotten as he stood there beside his cousin and best man, the Marquess of Milford Haven, both of them handsome in their uniforms.

The marriage service was conducted by the Archbishops of Canterbury and York and, as was then traditional, the bride promised to obey her husband as well as to love and honour him.

Left The scene in Westminster Abbey on 20 November 1947 as Princess Elizabeth leaves on the arm of her new husband. Behind them, carrying the bride's train, are the two pages, Prince William of Gloucester and Prince Michael of Kent, and the eight bridesmaids led by Princess Margaret and Princess Alexandra.

Below The newly created Duke of Edinburgh, handsome in his naval uniform, leads his radiant bride out of the Abbey to the sound of pealing bells. Her beautiful satin dress was woven in Dundee and embroidered with hundreds of tiny seed pearls by Norman Hartnell's patient seamstresses.

Above Amidst a shower of rose petals Lord and Lady Mountbatten and Princess Margaret give the couple an exciting send off as their coach leaves for Waterloo station and the honeymoon destination. Tucked in at the Princess's feet were her pet corgi Susan and two hot water bottles.

Below A wedding group photographed in the Throne Room at Buckingham Palace. As well as the bride's relatives and some of the groom's (it had not been thought diplomatic to invite his sisters because of their German connections), the guests included many representatives of the European royal houses.

Opposite Bride and groom photographed in the Throne Room at Buckingham Palace. The bride still carries her bouquet of white orchids, and the beauty of her long satin train with its pearl- and crystal-encrusted roses, stars and leaf fronds, is seen to its best advantage.

Opposite The second part of the royal honeymoon was spent at secluded Birkhall, the Jacobean mansion on the Balmoral estate lent them by the King, which in November 1947 was deep in snow. Princess Elizabeth soon found herself nursing a young husband with a severe cold.

Right Like any other newlyweds the royal couple are fascinated by their wedding photographs, sent down to them at Broadlands, the lovely Georgian house lent to them by Lord Mountbatten for the first part of their honeymoon.

Above The Drawing Room at Broadlands. Today it is the home of Lord and Lady Romsey, Lord Mountbatten's grandson and his wife, close friends of the Prince and Princess of Wales. Princess Elizabeth and the Duke of Edinburgh must have spent many happy honeymoon hours here.

After the ceremony there was the register to be signed and then a deep curtsey to be made to her parents and Queen Mary before the bride emerged on the arm of her new husband to the sound of abbey bells pealing and the tumultuous cheers of the crowds.

The honeymoon was intended to be a very private affair, but it seemed as if half the world's press photographers wanted to share their rural retreat in the New Forest. Broadlands, lent to them by Earl Mountbatten, was besieged and the little church at Romsey had never seen such crowds as appeared when the couple emerged from the Sunday service. True seclusion only came when the Princess and her husband moved up to Birkhall to spend the second half of their honeymoon on the Balmoral estate. Public curiosity

Left Public interest in the wedding was intense and to satisfy some of the curiosity the bride's clothes and 2,660 wedding gifts were put on display at St James's Palace in aid of charity. This is the picnic set which was a gift from Princess Margaret.

Opposite Clarence House in the Mall. Close to Buckingham Palace, it was Princess Elizabeth and the Duke of Edinburgh's first real home, though it was in such a dilapidated condition when it was offered to them that it was not ready for occupation until 4 July 1948.

Below The Garden Room at Clarence House as it looks today – the furnishings are those of the present occupant, the Queen Mother, Princess Elizabeth and her husband grew so fond of the house that they were reluctant to move back into Buckingham Palace when the Queen's accession seemed to demand it, but Winston Churchill was insistent.

was satisfied in one respect when the bride's gown and all the wedding gifts, including the beautiful sapphire and diamond necklace and bracelet from the King and a picnic set from Princess Margaret were put on display at St James's Palace in aid of charity.

Even royal newlyweds can find setting up home fraught with difficulties. To start with the Duke found himself living with his in-laws as he moved in to share the Princess's apartments at the Palace. Then the couple were offered Clarence House in the Mall, but it had been unoccupied for so long that it needed months of work to make it habitable, a task closely supervised by the couple themselves, who were determined that the finished result would reflect their tastes. Meanwhile a country house had become vacant at Windlesham Moor near Sunningdale in Berkshire and this seemed the ideal place to rent as it was close to Windsor, in good decorative order and had a large secluded garden. Princess Elizabeth was able to import into it many of her wedding presents and really begin to play the role of wife and home-maker. Temporary quarters were also found for the couple at Kensington Palace and at both houses they entertained family and friends to meals as any other young newlyweds might.

Prince Philip was far too active and enquiring to be idle for

Opposite **A beautifully romantic studio portrait of the Princess by Cecil Beaton. Even without the glitter of an evening dress she seems to have stepped straight out of the fairytale background. Pearls were and remain a favourite royal accessory, complementing the flawless complexion.**

Below **Mutual fascination as Princess Elizabeth makes eye contact with the mascot of the Welsh Regiment, splendidly decked out in ceremonial dress. Both were in Cardiff on 27 May 1948 when the royal lady was made the first Freewoman of the City.**

long and an appointment was soon found for him at the Admiralty. Weekends would be spent at Windlesham Moor, weekdays at Kensington, from where the Duke would drive his wife to Buckingham Palace before beginning his own busy working day.

At the Palace Princess Elizabeth continued her education in the affairs of state, seeing copies of the principal Foreign Office telegrams, even if she could not be shown secret cabinet documents. She went on performing the kind of official duties she had been undertaking before her marriage, making a particular effort to acquaint herself with the world of industry. It was a busy programme that had to be curtailed when news came that the upper floor of Clarence House was to be furnished as a nursery. Before the happy event occurred there were two very important occasions in the life of heiress and consort. The first came on St George's Day, 1948, when they were each invested as Knights of the Order of the Garter in a ceremony of great splendour at Windsor Castle. Admitting them to membership of the oldest surviving secular order of chivalry, six hundred years old that very year, was one of the greatest honours the King could bestow and he did it with great pride in his daughter.

That pride was justified by the splendid way she and her husband coped with their first official state visit to a foreign country, when the Princess captured all hearts in Paris later that year, addressing the people in their own language and with an accent which President Auriol declared better than his own. The occasion of the visit was the opening of an exhibition of Eight Centuries of British Life, but there was also a state banquet at the Elysée Palace and a gala performance at the Opéra to attend.

Above, left **The state visit of the royal couple to the French capital at Whitsun, 1948, aroused enormous interest amongst Parisians, who flocked in their thousands to catch even a fleeting glimpse. The Princess opened an Exhibition of Eight Centuries of British Life and made a dazzling appearance at the Paris Opéra with her husband.**

Below The Duke of Edinburgh's protective presence towers over his wife and their baby son, sleeping quietly in his Christening robe in the White Drawing Room at Buckingham Palace. The Duke was to miss much of his son's early development for he was posted to the Mediterranean Fleet in Malta in October 1949.

Above Great-grandmother, grandfather and mother pose proudly with the second in line of succession after his Christening at Buckingham Palace. Prince Charles was born there a month earlier, on 14 November 1948. 'I still can't believe he is really mine', the Princess wrote to a friend soon afterwards.

Once back home, the Princess found herself enjoying a very much quieter life. Not only did her public appearances cease for a while, but she also became something of a Navy widow, for Prince Philip embarked on a six-month course at Greenwich which entailed his being quartered in the barracks there and only meeting his wife at weekends. Elizabeth did the sensible thing and spent most of her time with the rest of her family, both at Buckingham Palace and on their annual holiday at Balmoral. It was therefore under her parents' roof that she gave birth to her first child. Shortly after 9.15 on the evening of 14 November word went round the crowd who had been waiting outside the Palace all day that a baby boy had been delivered. Blue-eyed and fair-haired, he weighed a healthy 7lbs 6oz, and a month and a day later was to be christened Charles Philip Arthur George. By the King's direction there was this time no Home Secretary waiting in an adjoining room even though this child was now second in the line of succession. It was also due to the King's foresight that Charles was born a Prince, for a proclamation had been issued declaring that all children of this Princess should have such rank.

Prince Charles spent his earliest months at Windlesham Moor, for it was not until 4 July, or 'Independence Day' as Prince Philip described it, that Clarence House was finally ready for occupation. Though Princess Elizabeth spent much of her time in the nursery, Prince Philip had little opportunity to enjoy watching his young son's development. In October 1949 he was posted to the Mediterranean Fleet, which had its headquarters in Malta. Princess Elizabeth was able to fly out there for holidays with her husband and they were together for Christmas 1949, Prince Charles having been left in the care of his doting grandparents and aunt. The Princess was back in time for the Derby of 1950, but her programme of public engagements had soon to be curtailed again, this time in the interests of the little Princess who was born on 15 August. Anne Elizabeth Alice Louise was born at Clarence House at 11.50 a.m. and news of her arrival was telephoned by her proud father, home on leave from Malta, to an equally proud grandfather, on holiday at

Opposite, top **Leaving her baby son in the care of his doting grandparents and aunt, the Princess was able to visit her husband in Malta at the end of 1949 and stayed at the beautiful Villa Guardamangia.**

Below **The young Prince Charles is being introduced to the large secluded garden of Windlesham Moor, the rented house near Windsor where his parents spent part of their early married life.**

Right **In October 1949 Princess Elizabeth discovered what a Council house drawing room looks like when she visited this Ilford family in the company of the local Mayor and the Lord Lieutenant of Essex.**

Right, bottom A cat may look at a king, but a dog may look at a Home Secretary instead. Mr Chuter Ede seems amused by this gatecrasher at the ceremony welcoming the royal couple to Sark in 1949.

Balmoral. All the family were at the Palace for the Christening on 21 October, the toddler Prince Charles stealing the scene at Cecil Beaton's photographic session afterwards.

The Princess continued to divide her loyalties between children and husband, managing to spend a fair amount of time in the villa which the couple had rented in Valetta. The Prince's posting was good excuse for a few tourist visits, to Athens to stay with the Greek King and Queen and to view not only the Parthenon but also some of the sights of her husband's youth, then in April 1951 to the British Embassy in Rome. A walk round the Forum brought the world of the ancient Romans alive, while news of her brief private visit to Pope Pius XII sparked off some lively debates at home.

In 1951 Britain was trying to shake off the troubles of the immediate past and looking to the brave new world symbolised by the Festival of Britain, with its Dome of Discovery and Skylon on London's South Bank. The Royal Family were all enthusiastic visitors, but the excitement perhaps distracted attention from the fact that the King was becoming a very sick man. So sick was he that the Princess was being asked to take on more and more of his duties. She deputised for him during King Haakon of Norway's state

Above **On 4 May 1951 Princess Elizabeth and the Duke of Edinburgh visited London's South Bank with the rest of the Royal Family to enjoy the excitement of the Festival of Britain. In the background here is the Royal Festival Hall, one of the few surviving reminders of the new sense of optimism the Festival brought.**

Page 88 **Prince Philip was home on leave from Malta when his young daughter made her first appearance on 15 August 1950. Anne Elizabeth Alice Louise was born at her parents' home, Clarence House, but christened at Buckingham Palace.**

Page 89 **Karsh of Ottawa took this photograph of Princess Elizabeth in July 1951. Wearing her first and favourite tiara, she is seated in one of the rooms at Clarence House, against a simple setting designed not to distract from the splendour of her gown.**

Left The Duke of Edinburgh pulls a face for the entertainment of his young daughter in the grounds of Clarence House. This happy photograph is one of a series taken in 1951 at the London home to which the family had become particularly attached.

Below Wearing a dream of a dress in romantic lace and tulle, the Princess poses with her husband for the camera of Baron. Her beautiful pearl and diamond diadem was originally made for King George IV and it is the one she always wears on her way to the State Opening of Parliament.

Above A truly radiant Princess is the delighted recipient of a toy cooking stove, a somewhat enlightened gift for her two-year-old son in the days before women's liberation. She was a guest at the 1951 Flower Ball at the Savoy Hotel in London on 22 May 1951. Behind the Princess is Lieutenant Michael Parker, RN, Prince Philip's close friend and Private Secretary.

Opposite A tiny ballerina, the 'baby' of the Royal Winnipeg Ballet, executes a perfect curtsey as she presents a bouquet to Princess Elizabeth after the royal couple had watched a performance given in their honour during their tour of Canada in October 1951.

Below If the Princess had ever had a childhood ambition to be an engine-driver it was fulfilled at the end of October 1951 when she took over the controls of the Royal Train as it carried her and Prince Philip to a rousing welcome at Edmonton in Alberta.

visit and for the second year running took the King's place at the Trooping the Colour ceremony, this time elegantly dressed in scarlet jacket and dark riding skirt as Colonel-in-Chief of the Grenadier Guards.

At this point Prince Philip felt obliged to abandon his naval career indefinitely and was thrown back into the round of royal duties with a vengeance as the couple flew out to Ottawa on 8 October for a gruelling tour of Canada. They made such a glamorous pair as they journeyed around by train, waving to the cheering crowds from the observation platform, that press coverage was phenomenal. Everyone wanted to shake the royal hands and on some days there were as many as thirteen functions to attend. If there were highlights that made the tour different, perhaps these were the visits to Niagara Falls, to a rodeo at Calgary – where it was so cold that the royal couple had to be wrapped in blankets to watch

Above After the warmest of welcomes in Canada there was equal enthusiasm when the royal couple moved on to Washington for a short visit. President Truman raises some smiles as he thanks the Princess for presenting to him on the King's behalf the gold-framed overmantel picture and mirror and the ancient candlesticks standing behind him. Mrs Truman looks on.

Opposite The Queen's dresser had to dash out to a Canadian department store to buy this swinging skirt for her to wear at an impromptu square dance at Government House in Ottawa during the 1951 tour. Prince Philip sported a check shirt and jeans, still with their price tag, for the occasion.

it – and to a square dance. For the latter the Queen's dresser had to be hurriedly dispatched to the shops to find the boldly patterned full skirt which swung its way round Government House and on to the front pages of newspapers round the world the following day.

The reception was hardly less enthusiastic in Washington where, under the tightest security, the couple met President Truman during a two-day visit and managed to shake about 1,600 hands at a British Embassy reception. All in all they could look back with triumph as they waved goodbye at St John, New Brunswick, and sailed for home. There was no doubt in Winston Churchill's mind as he expressed the nation's thanks at a welcoming home banquet at the Guildhall.

There had been reassuring news about the King's health while they were away, but he was still not fit enough to undertake a planned tour of New Zealand and Australia early in 1952. It was decided that the Princess and her husband should go instead, but first they were to have a short holiday in Kenya where the King hoped they would experience that delight he had felt when he saw his first big game in the wild. Looking tired and haggard, he waved the pair goodbye from the tarmac of a chilly London Airport at noon on 31 January.

It was not a total break from official engagements for, within hours of arrival, the Princess was visiting a maternity hospital and there was a garden party to attend before she was allowed to escape to the wildlife parks and become the watcher instead of the watched. First there was the excitement of seeing dik-diks and a lion with its kill in Nairobi National Park, then it was off to Sagana Lodge, Nyeri, a cedarwood bungalow presented by the Kenyan people on the occasion of her wedding. From there the couple made an excursion to Treetops, the famous hotel thirty feet above ground in a giant fig tree. The Princess and the Duke arrived in the midst of what could have been a frightening elephant invasion, and then stayed up half the night to watch rhinos on a floodlit salt lick.

There was no inkling that this was to be Elizabeth's last night as a Princess, and even as she went off to fish with her husband in the morning she was unaware of what much of the rest of the world already knew. During the night her father had passed quietly away in his sleep at Sandringham. The news reached Nairobi through a Reuter newsagency flash and was passed on to the Princess's private secretary by a local reporter. It was left to Prince Philip to tell his young wife that she had seen her father for the last time. In spite of the shocking suddenness of it all the new Queen acted in her sorrow with calm dignity. Arrangements were rapidly made to fly the couple back to London and their plane was touching down at London Airport in the late afternoon of 7 February. A row of sombre-suited privy counsellors and ministers was lined up to pay homage to the young Queen as the solitary black-coated figure, touchingly beautiful in her grief, emerged from the plane and descended the gangway. It was an unforgettably poignant moment.

The couple were driven to Clarence House, where Queen Mary was waiting to kiss her grand-daughter's hand in homage and share her sorrow in the loss of a loved one. There were others at Sandringham to grieve with, but affairs of state soon pressed upon the new Queen. Most immediately instructions had to be given to the Earl Marshal, the Duke of Norfolk, about her father's funeral. Then there was the Queen's first Privy Council, held at St James's Palace the following morning, at which she declared: 'I shall always work, as my father did throughout his reign, to uphold the constitutional Government and to advance the happiness and prosperity of my peoples, spread as they are the world over... I pray that God will help me to discharge worthily this heavy task that has been laid upon me so early in my life.' Her words, and the quiet dignity with which they were uttered, inspired those present with a great optimism for the new reign.

Back at Clarence House the Queen watched her Proclamation on television before journeying down to Sandringham to comfort her mother and sister. The King's body was removed to London to lie in state in Westminster Hall where over a quarter of a million people filed past to pay their respects. The funeral itself was held at St George's Chapel, Windsor, on 15 February, with three veiled Queens in mourning – mother, wife and daughter. And so, in the words of Tennyson's dying King Arthur, himself born away by three black-robed lamenting queens, 'The old order changeth, yielding place to new', or in the herald's more ruthless recognition of life's continuity, 'The King is dead. Long live the Queen.'

Above A sad homecoming for the new Queen. After an overnight flight from Kenya a solitary black-coated figure descends from the aircraft to be greeted by the Prime Minister Winston Churchill, Mr Attlee, leader of the Opposition, and a row of sombre-suited privy counsellors and ministers.

Top Last days as a Princess. This little Kenyan boy, named Prince because he was born on the same day as Prince Charles, shyly refuses to hand over his bouquet and has to have a little coaxing from the Princess. She had just arrived in Nairobi for what should have been the start of a round-the-world tour but was cut short by the tragic death of the King on 6 February 1952.

Opposite United in their grief, three Queens mourn the passing of a son, a husband and a father as they await the arrival of the King's coffin at Westminster Hall for the lying-in-state.

VIVAT REGINA!

The strains of the day nearly over, the main actors in the drama can relax on the balcony of Buckingham Palace as the crowds gather for a last glimpse of the Queen in her coronation robes. Princess Anne is at last able to have a part in her mother's big day.

The new Queen hardly had time to reflect on the heavy burden that had been thrust upon her so prematurely, for there were papers to be signed, appointments to be approved and a steady stream of mourners to be received. As their new Head, she was also required to give audiences for the Commonwealth ministers and High Commissioners then in London as well as for her British ministers. Ceremonies which her father had planned to attend now fell to her lot, so that she found herself officiating at her first investiture in March 1952, when fifty-one new knights were created at Buckingham Palace. Her first official function beyond its walls was at Westminster Abbey in April when, still in mourning, she distributed the first Maundy Money of the new reign.

Every part of the kingdom longed to pay homage to the Queen. She did her best to make it possible, undertaking one hundred and forty engagements in five months and visiting places as far apart as Edinburgh and Devon. Her first real break for relaxation did not come until two months into her reign when she was able to join the Duke and Duchess of Beaufort at Badminton House to watch the Horse Trials known as the Three-day Event.

Opposite As Princess, Elizabeth had attended many race meetings, and with growing enthusiasm. On 17 June 1952 she made her first visit as Queen to the opening meeting of Royal Ascot and she seems to be enjoying every minute to judge from the smiling face in the middle of the Royal Box.

Below The first public engagement of the new Queen. Still in mourning, she leaves Westminster Abbey after distributing Maundy Money on 10 April 1952. Her guard of honour is provided by the Yeomen of the Guard and even some of the gentlemen in the procession carry nosegays, a practice dating back to the days when the capital's smells were far from savoury!

The new First Family had grown so attached to their Clarence House home that they cherished the forlorn hope of staying on there and using Buckingham Palace just as an official residence. Prime Minister Churchill was adamant that it would not do, however, and so after the customary Easter spent at Windsor they moved on 5 May to join the Queen Mother. It was to be an exchange of homes for within the year she and Princess Margaret had left to take up residence at Clarence House.

Below, left A pensive moment in 1952, but already the young Queen seems assured in her new role. She was fortunate to have by her side on most public appearances a supportive and understanding husband who already had his own distinguished record of service to his adopted country, though events had forced him to abandon his naval career.

Right A radiant smile captured for ever by a lucky press photographer. His vigilance after the Queen's first State Opening of Parliament in 1952 was rewarded with a photograph that was to appear in homes and offices around the world.

Opposite, right Continuing in the tradition established by her grandfather, Queen Elizabeth makes her first Christmas broadcast. It was transmitted live from Sandringham, the private royal home in Norfolk which was for long the scene of Christmas festivities until superceded by Windsor Castle.

Below On 3 December 1952 the Queen gave the first big party of her reign, entertaining the Commonwealth prime ministers and their wives to dinner at Buckingham Palace. Among the premiers present were two particularly distinguished older statesmen, Winston Churchill and Robert Menzies of Australia, standing next to the Queen in this commemorative photograph.

Pages 104–105 Cecil Beaton's famous photograph of the newly crowned Queen in her coronation regalia. She wears the Imperial State Crown and carries the Sovereign's Orb and the Sceptre with the Cross. Her white satin gown, designed by Norman Hartnell, is encrusted with precious and semi-precious stones, and over it is draped the purple velvet Imperial Robe of State.

There were remaining in that first year two important events at which the Queen would play the role so recently her father's. One was the State Opening of Parliament, at which she appeared resplendent in a golden dress draped with Queen Victoria's Parliamentary mantle and wearing the former Queen's diadem. It was perhaps the relief at another task performed impeccably that made her look so radiant in the coach driving back to the Palace. It was a radiance captured for ever by a watchful press photographer, rewarded with a picture which was soon in millions of homes and offices throughout the land. Back on the Palace balcony the rest of the day belonged to three-year-old Prince Charles, making his first appearance there with his sister to the delight of the crowds assembled below.

Also in November there was a reunion with Commonwealth premiers and delegates to the Commonwealth Conference at a state dinner given for them at Buckingham Palace. As the King's deputy and understudy she had met many of them before and she would be meeting them again and again in the years to come, not only in London but during the countless tours she was to undertake. Though less than half the age of most of them the young Queen looked happy and relaxed as she posed for the group photograph, a diminutive but glamorous figure amidst the dinner jackets.

The formal events were perhaps good practice for the ceremonial of the Coronation, appointed for June of the next year though planning had been going on under the control of the Duke of Norfolk since almost immediately after the King's death. The Queen had her own step-by-step rehearsals in the Palace Ballroom and Picture Gallery, practising with particular care the art of walking with the 8lb St Edward's Crown on her head. Norman Hartnell designed the dress for this historic occasion, incorporating beautiful embroidered versions of the national emblems, the Tudor rose, the thistle of Scotland, the Welsh leek and the Irish shamrock. It was the Queen who insisted that he add the emblems of the Dominions as well. The result was splendidly appropriate to the occasion.

The second of June, 1953, dawned wet and overcast, but nothing could dampen the enthusiasm of the crowd, twenty deep in places and often weary from an all-night wait on the hard pavements. The excited sense of expectation was heightened when news filtered through that the world's highest mountain had been climbed for the first time and by a British expedition. Sherpa Tensing and New Zealander Edmund Hillary had made their own uniquely memorable contribution to what seemed the dawning of a new Elizabethan age.

For millions of televison viewers, watching at home on their tiny pioneer black and white sets, and for those fortunate enough to be seated near the throne in Westminster Abbey, the abiding image of the day was of the young Queen's solitary but somehow mystical figure isolated amidst the splendour of pomp and ceremony around her. Many minds must have harked back to the pleas made in her first Christmas broadcast from Sandringham: 'Pray for me on that day. . . . Pray that God may give me wisdom and strength to carry out the solemn promises that I shall be making, and that I may faithfully serve Him and you all the days of my life.'

The crowning was not, alas, a moment which the Queen's grandmother had lived to see, for Queen Mary, insisting as she grew more frail that her death should not be allowed to postpone the Coronation, had passed away ten weeks earlier. But her great-grandson, thought too young to sit quietly through the entire service, was brought in to the Royal Gallery before the anointing to sit between his aunt and his grandmother, plying them with the questions of a curious four-year-old.

The supreme moment came as the Archbishop of Canterbury raised St Edward's Crown high in the air and then lowered it on to the young Queen's head. A great cry of acclamation went up. Princes and princesses, peers and peeresses, as if with one voice, shouted 'God save the Queen.' First to pay homage, in poetic words of ancient lineage, was her husband: 'I, Philip, Duke of Edinburgh, do become your liege man of life and limb, and of earthly worship, and faith and truth I will bear unto you. . . .'

When the ceremony was over the Queen, wearing now the lighter Imperial State Crown and bearing in one hand the Orb, symbol of Christian rule, and in the other the Sceptre with the Cross, processed through the Abbey, supported on either side by two of her Archbishops and with six maids of honour bearing her long train. Accompanied back to the Palace by the Duke of Edinburgh in the splendid gold coach, she had some radiant smiles for those waiting patiently by the roadside in the rain.

Another Queen who had starred briefly in the Coronation procession was nineteen-stone (266-lb) Salote of Tonga, who

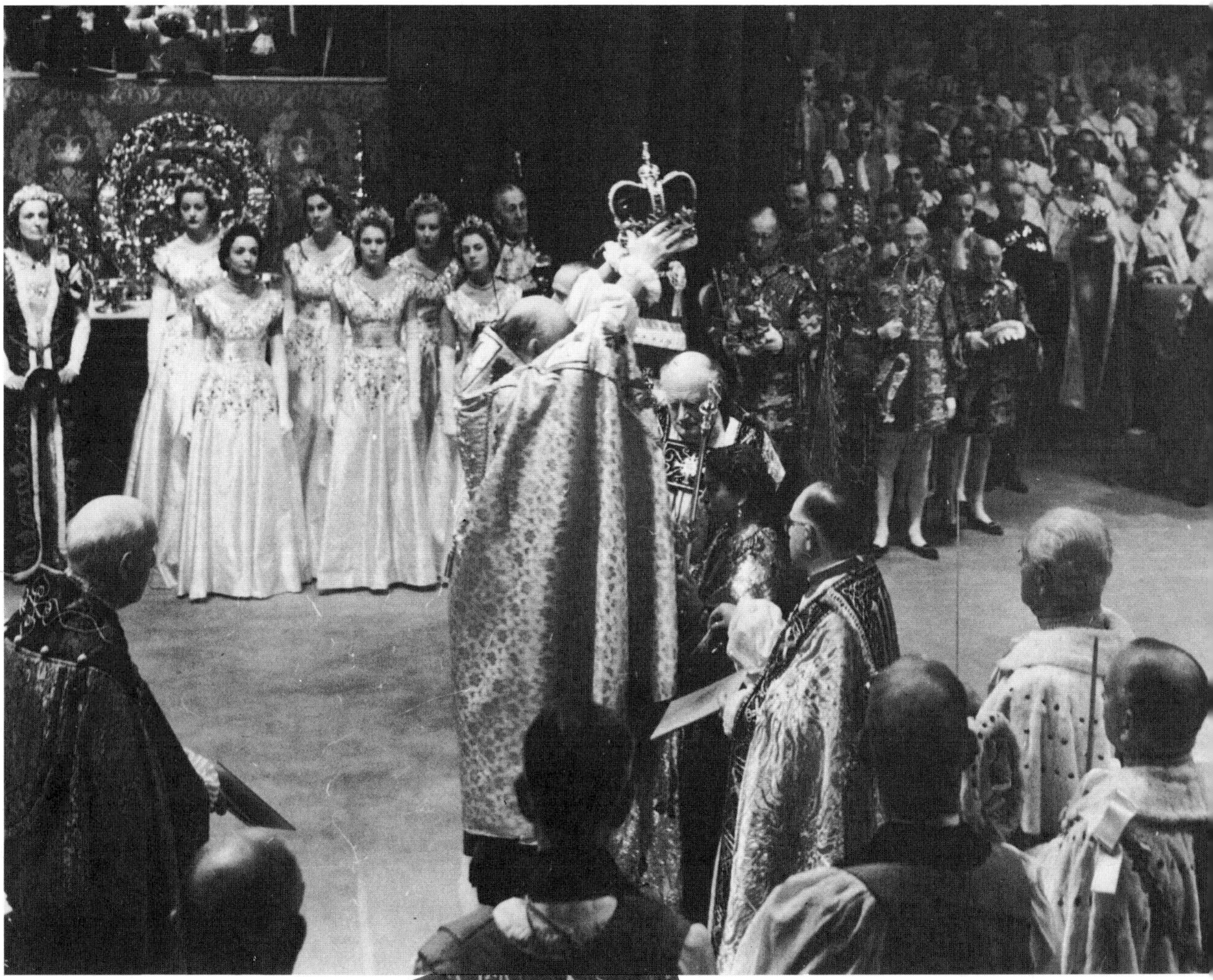

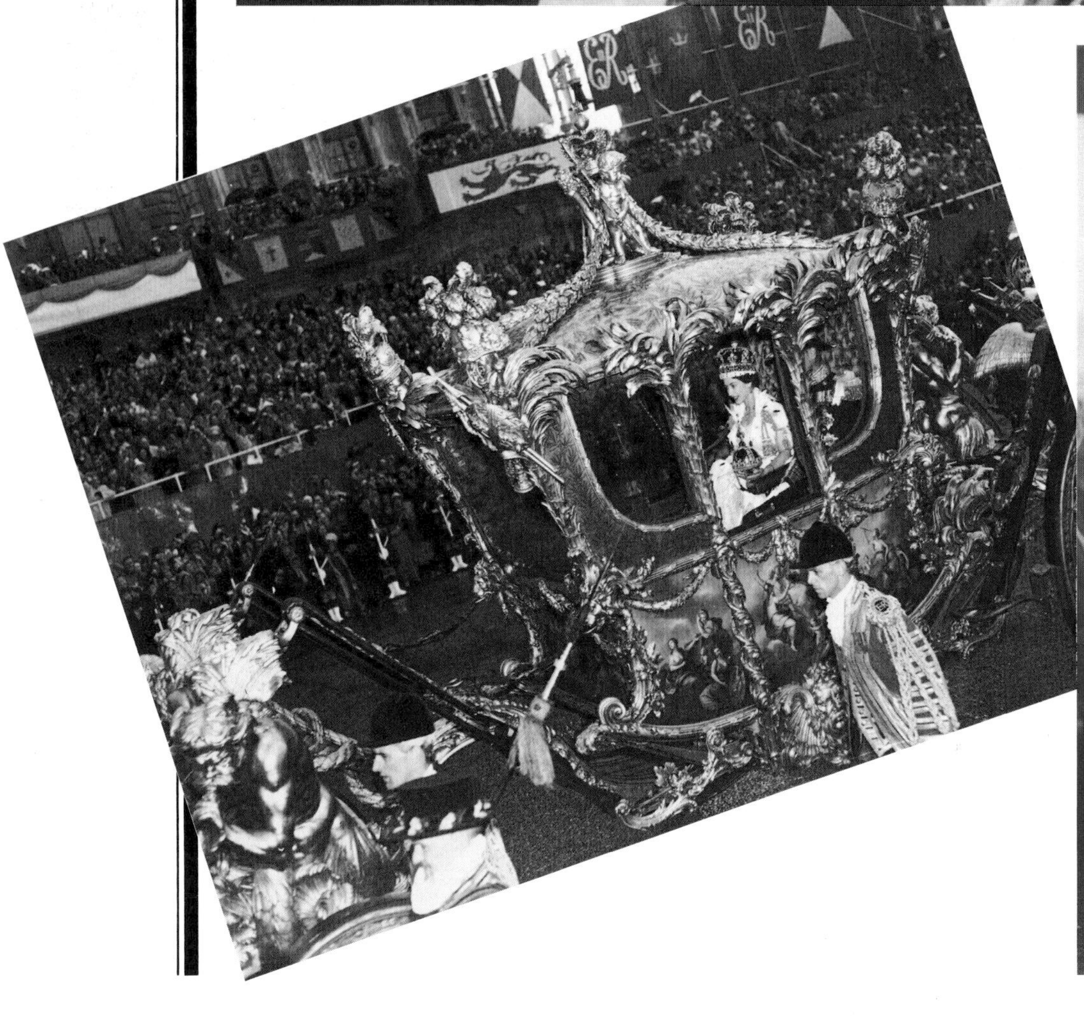

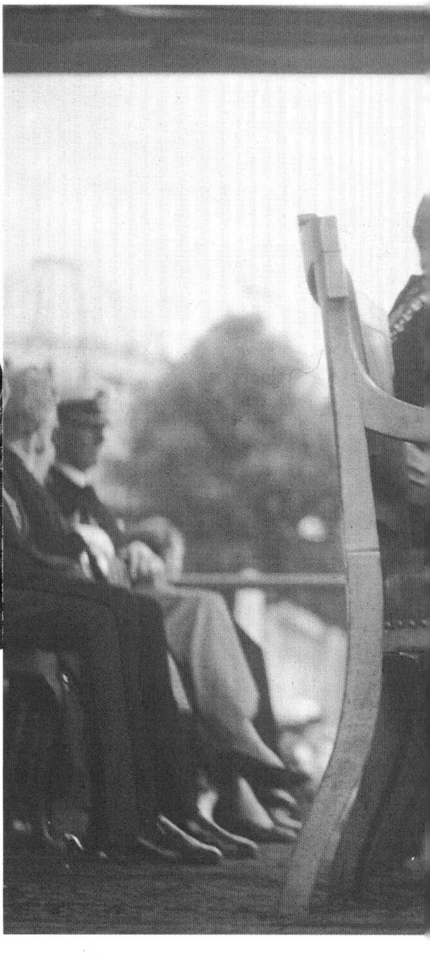

Opposite, top The supreme moment of the coronation on 2 June 1953. The Archbishop of Canterbury holds aloft St Edward's Crown before reverently lowering it on to the young Queen's head.

Opposite, bottom, left Seated in the magnificent Gold State Coach for the ride back to Buckingham Palace from the Abbey, the newly crowned Queen presents a radiant picture for the rain-soaked crowds, many of whom had waited overnight on the hard pavements to experience this moment of history.

Right Leaving Bermuda's House of Assembly in Hamilton, seat of the Commonwealth's oldest parliament outside Westminster. Bermuda was the first port of call on the Commonwealth Tour and the royal couple arrived there on 24 November, to receive a rousing welcome.

Below Anxious to be seen by as many of her subjects as possible in this coronation year of 1953, the young Queen was in Wales only a month after her crowning, to watch one of the many displays put on in her honour. The special place of the Principality in royal affections was to be acknowledged five years later when the Queen created her eldest son Prince of Wales.

refused to have the roof raised over her carriage against the rain and who smiled broadly to one and all. She was to be one of the hosts during the Commonwealth Tour which commenced in November. The tour was to cover in reverse order much of the ground planned for that ill-fated 1952 tour. First port of call was Bermuda, where the royal plane touched down on 24 November to allow the royal couple to visit the Commonwealth's oldest parliament outside Westminster and be seen by thousands of cheering children.

The Caribbean proved a delightful surprise as they drove across a Jamaica full of gay and colourful people, luscious fruit and flowers and never-ending calypso serenades. The Queen's letters home to Princess Margaret were so full of its praises that they sparked off in the younger sister a curiosity to see it for herself which was to end with an abiding love for one of the Caribbean's gems, the island of Mustique.

From Jamaica's Kingston the royal party sailed in the liner *Gothic* for the islands of the Pacific. Unwisely as it turned out, the Queen and the Duke went ashore at Colon as their ship entered the Panama Canal and in their separate cars were so mobbed by the crowds that they had to be rescued and reunited by the police. There was a welcome and well-earned rest as their journey continued lazily across the blue Pacific towards Fiji and then Tonga, where Queen Salote returned the Coronation hospitality and the couple met the islands' oldest inhabitant, a giant tortoise purported to have been alive when Captain Cook landed there.

Next on the itinerary was a five-week visit to New Zealand where 'The Rare White Heron of the Single Flight', as the Maoris called her, delivered her Christmas broadcast. Newspapers and magazines at home were full of news of the tour and the Queen's fashions were followed with particular interest. No royal tour before had covered so much ground – in Australia alone 10,000 miles by air, 2,500 miles by road and 900 miles by train, with hardly more than a week's worth of rest days in two months. Novelty was provided by visits to the Great Barrier Reef, to a flying doctor station and to see some of the staples of the Australian economy at cattle stations and sheep shows.

Left A triumphant homecoming from the Commonwealth Tour on 15 May 1954. In an open State landau escorted by a Sovereign's Escort of the Household Cavalry the Queen and the Duke of Edinburgh, accompanied by their two children, are driven up Whitehall towards Buckingham Palace, the home they had not seen since November.

Above After the coronation visits to Scotland, Northern Ireland and Wales it was the turn of the Commonwealth. Towards the end of the year the royal couple set off on a six-month tour which was to take them round the world. Much of their travelling was on board the liner *Gothic* from which the royal couple were able to make their own photographic record of the ceremonies that marked their arrival and departure.

After Australia there was a brief trip to the Cocos Islands, then eleven days in Ceylon where they experienced the greatest spectacle of the tour as one hundred and twenty-five decorated elephants and a thousand whirling dancers paraded before them in the Raja Perahera ceremony. It was an event enjoyed too by *Gothic*'s acting Master of the Household, Viscount Althorp, before he was allowed to fly home early to be with his future bride, Frances Roche, now best known as the Princess of Wales's mother.

The royal couple had plans for a reunion of their own before they got home. Sailing for Malta aboard the newly launched Royal Yacht *Britannia* were Prince Charles and Princess Anne, who were delighted when their parents joined them at Tobruk in Libya, enabling the family to share a triumphant homecoming as the Royal Yacht sailed up the Thames and into the Pool of London. There was a jet flypast in their honour and a line-up of Ministers to greet the Queen, who proceeded by royal barge to Westminster Pier and thence to the Palace. The following week the City offered its welcome home with a lunch at the Guildhall and not long after that there was a reunion with a fellow-traveller when the royal couple were guests at the wedding of their eldest son's future in-laws!

Early in the following year it was Princess Margaret's turn to discover those Caribbean delights described by her sister. She needed a temporary respite from the difficulties which seemed to be looming for her at home. Back in Coronation year there had been rumours in the Continental and American press that a romance was developing between the Princess and Group Captain Peter Townsend, one of that select group of young war heroes chosen to be personal Equerries by the late King. By 1953 he had become Comptroller of Clarence House and was almost treated as one of the family by his royal employers. It was only natural that in 1952, the year of her great loss, Princess Margaret should have turned for comfort to this older man and found in him perhaps some substitute for her father's caring presence. It was at Windsor the following year, when by chance left alone together in the Red Drawing Room, that they declared their mutual love. When news of it was broken to the Queen she was sympathetic, but found herself in an impossible situation. Much as she liked Peter Townsend, he was a divorced man and she was head of a Church whose canon forbade divorce. As Defender of the Faith she could hardly assent to her sister's marriage to this man.

All the family fervently hoped for some painless outcome and various authorities were consulted in the hope of finding a way out. Group Captain Townsend meanwhile accepted a posting to Brussels as an air attaché so that the strength of the couple's love might be tested by a trial separation. Back in Britain from her triumphant Caribbean tour, the Princess remained as committed in her affections as she had ever been. There seemed a little hope when Sir Winston Churchill, now in his eighty-first year, resigned as Prime Minister and a remarried divorcé, Sir Anthony Eden, was chosen to succeed him. But there was one rule for commoners, another for royalty, and Eden had to warn the Princess that her proposed marriage would mean the renunciation of her royal rights,

Above The Queen paid her first Prime Minister the highest of compliments by dining with him at 10 Downing Street, the night before his resignation from office. Just before midnight on 4 April 1955 Sir Winston Churchill, her delighted host, said farewell to the young monarch whom he admired so much.

Opposite Even back in 1955 five-year-old Princess Anne looked as if she knew exactly what she was doing when it came to dealing with horses. Here she helps her mother adjust a pony's bridle during one of their happy family holidays at Balmoral. The Princess learnt to ride when she was only three.

functions and income. She had also to consider the distress which would be caused to her family. In the end, after several agonising meetings with the Group Captain, home from Brussels, the statement was issued that 'mindful of the Church's teaching', the Princess had 'decided not to marry Group Captain Townsend'.

Blessed with a happy marriage herself, the Queen was only too well aware of the support to be gained from a loving and understanding spouse. That is not to say that Prince Philip has ever found his position easy. It was particularly difficult after the Queen's accession. He suddenly found himself playing very much second fiddle. Staff would go to the Queen for decisions about everything, heaping more burdens on to already overloaded shoulders. Prince Philip determined to do all in his power to lighten his wife's load by taking upon himself any of the tasks he might reasonably fulfil. He kept himself well abreast of current affairs and took an informed interest in what might be considered the more masculine aspects of society, thus keeping himself in a good position to advise his wife when need be.

It has been a godsend for the Queen to have the Duke by her side during overseas tours – and there was another important one in 1956, this time to Nigeria, then largest of the colonies. Two Nigerian equerries were appointed to the Royal Household to ensure that everything undertaken fulfilled African expectations. At the Lagos garden party the Duke was careful to guide his wife in the direction of black Africans rather than the white settlers with whom she might initially have felt most at home. It was a boost for multi-racialism which did not pass unnoticed. Her well-publicised visit to the Oji River leper settlement, where the couple met sufferers of all conditions and adopted financially two leper children, did much to lessen African fear of the disease's contagion. On the lighter side, providing one of the highlights of the visit were the eight thousand mounted warriors who staged a magnificently spectacular Durbar at the northern town of Kaduna.

Above **The Queen inspects a guard of honour during her state visit to Nigeria at the beginning of 1956. While there the royal couple visited a leper settlement and adopted financially two leper children, doing much thereby to lessen African fear of the disease.**

Above The young Queen wears another of her beautiful jewel-encrusted evening dresses in this charming mid-fifties portrait. The tiara is one of her favourites and very versatile because the emerald drops can be replaced with pearls. As so often in formal portraits, she wears the Star of the Order of the Garter, the premier Order of Chivalry.

Very much a modern prince, anxious that the monarchy should move with the times though not ahead of them, Prince Philip encouraged some changes at Court. In 1956 the first of many informal Buckingham Palace luncheons was given, during which Queen and consort chat to seven or eight guests chosen for their distinction in a variety of walks of life, and in the following year it was announced that there would be no more presentation parties for debutantes. The old formal garden parties at the Palace gave way to Commonwealth gatherings of up to seven thousand, which did much to promote international understanding and enhance the Queen's position as Head of the Commonwealth.

Above, left In May 1957 there was a state visit to Denmark where the hosts were King Frederik and Queen Ingrid, here seen waving from a balcony with their royal guests. The Queen and the Duke of Edinburgh undoubtedly appreciated the informal friendliness of the Scandinavians.

Opposite, top Danish and British flags are flying in celebration as the Queen steps out of her carriage for her first visit as monarch to Denmark. King Frederik (right) managed to maintain his cheerful hospitality in spite of a recent back injury brought on by his hobby of weightlifting.

Left The bond between the Dutch and British monarchs is a strong one so a state visit to the Netherlands in March 1958 was very agreeable for the Queen. Her delight is plain to see in this charming photograph.

Below For her visit in April 1957 to the capital of the fashion world the Queen wore some sparkling creations which drew gasps of admiration from Parisians. Here she is seen arriving at the British Embassy in Paris where she gave a reception for President Coty.

Above During her state visit to the Netherlands the Queen bestowed the Order of the Garter on her hostess Queen Juliana, here seen making a balcony appearance with her royal guests and husband Prince Bernhard. The Queen's father had bestowed the same honour on the Dutch Queen's mother, Queen Wilhelmina, during her wartime exile in Britain in 1944.

In view of the powerful influence the Duke was exerting, it was particularly unfortunate that the Press, ever anxious to create a scandal, decided to invent a rift between the couple. The flames of this rumour were fuelled by another of the Prince's absences abroad, this time to open the 1956 Olympic Games in Melbourne. An accident of Australian planning meant that the Duke had to miss spending his wedding anniversary with his wife. He also missed being on hand with advice during the Suez crisis and when ill-health forced the resignation of Anthony Eden and a successor had to be appointed. Of course she consulted leading statesmen, but ultimately it was Harold Macmillan, not Rab Butler, who was summoned to the Palace, the Queen under instruction having chosen the leader of Government thought most acceptable to Parliament.

Prince Philip meanwhile was still aboard *Britannia* on his way back from Australia, having spent much of his four months away visiting remote islands such as the Falklands and the Galapagos. The Queen flew out to join him for a quiet spring weekend reunion in Portugal before the pair began a three-day state visit. Later in the year her feelings for him and gratitude for his services to the Commonwealth were expressed in the bestowal of the title 'Prince of the United Kingdom' – he had till then been only a duke.

In October the Queen had her first ordeal by live television when she broadcast to the Canadian people from Ottawa before appearing in her Coronation dress to open their parliament. The producer noticed 'congealed terror' in her eyes, but managed to dispel this with an instruction passed on from Prince Philip to 'remember the wailing and gnashing of teeth'!

Lost by her ancestor George III, American hearts were to be recaptured at Jamestown during celebrations for the 350th anniversary of the founding of Virginia, and again in New York, where the couple received the traditional Broadway welcome as well as a standing ovation from delegates to the United Nations.

The success of her Canadian broadcast persuaded the Queen to give her 1957 Christmas message on television. It had to be broadcast live, again creating a tension in the Queen, which caused her to miss most of her Christmas lunch. Only when she thought it was all over did she relax and flash a radiant smile of relief at her watching husband, for all the world to see!

Though she spent as much time with her children as she could, the Queen was away so much that a particularly heavy burden fell upon the Scottish-born nannies and governess, who insisted on strict discipline and no spoiling. Prince Charles was now reaching the age when important decisions had to be made about his educational future. In line with the Duke's general ideas about modernising the monarchy, it was decided to send him away to school and so it was that at the age of eight he arrived at Hill House day school in Knightsbridge, one with a good mixture of boys from all the neighbouring embassies and homes. Princes Charles did well in history, French and geography, and showed some athletic prowess at the school's summer sports day when his family turned up to cheer him on.

The first heir to the Throne to be educated away from home, the young Prince was easy prey for pressman while in London, and it was hoped that when he moved to Prince Philip's old boarding school, Cheam in Hampshire, he might be left alone by the media. The Queen went so far as to issue a statement asking 'that Prince Charles shall be treated the same as other boys'. It seemed a vain

Above Not a view of the Royal Family that one often sees. The Queen and her children are watching a polo match at Smith's Lawn, Windsor, though the interest of the two royal ladies has temporarily shifted. Polo was a favourite sport of Prince Philip, whose enthusiasm for it was to be inherited by his eldest son.

Left The Queen and Prince Philip come ashore from the Royal Yacht *Britannia* at Wolfe's Cove, Quebec City, at the start of their royal visit to Canada in 1959. On 26 June the Queen and President Eisenhower were to formally open the St Lawrence Seaway.

hope as newspaper after newspaper published articles about Charles and his school. In the end a press conference was called at which the Queen's press secretary pointed out that she would have to remove her son from the school if the publicity continued. The strategy seemed to work, though it was difficult to treat 'as other boys' a child who in his first year at the school heard his mother declaring him Prince of Wales in a recording played to the crowds at the closing ceremony of the Commonwealth Games in Cardiff.

There was another big event in store for Prince Charles, and there were inklings of what it might be during the Queen's visit to Canada in 1959 to open the St Lawrence Seaway in the company of President and Mrs Eisenhower. Few guessed why she should have found the six-week tour particularly strenuous and why illness forced her to cancel some of her engagements. It was not until her return home that it was announced that she was expecting her third child the following February. Andrew Albert Christian Edward duly arrived on the nineteenth, separated by ten years from his sister. By the Queen's prior declaration Prince Andrew was the first of her offspring whose descendants would bear the name 'Mountbatten-Windsor'.

Above **The Queen and the Duke welcomed a new member of their 'second family' on 19 February 1960 when Prince Andrew was born.**

Bottom, right **The Queen saw her first Derby while still a Princess and has been an enthusiastic attender ever since. Here she is at the 1960 Derby with three other royal ladies, her aunts the Princess Royal and Princess Marina, Duchess of Kent, and the Queen Mother.**

Right **Covent Garden was in festive mood on the night of 19 October 1960 when the Queen took her guests the King and Queen of Nepal to a gala performance.**

Bottom, left **London was honoured by a state visit from President de Gaulle in April 1960. During the war he had directed French resistance from exile in England so the visit must have stirred many memories.**

Good news did not come singly, for later in the month it was announced that Princess Margaret would marry the royal photographer, Antony Armstrong-Jones. They seemed a well-matched couple with their shared interest in the arts and the Princess made a stunningly beautiful bride as she stood at the altar in Westminster Abbey later in the year, with Princess Anne in attendance as one of the bridesmaids. For the Queen it was a delight to see an end to her sister's years of loneliness and heartache, and when the letters started to arrive describing the deserted beaches of their Caribbean honeymoon it seemed as if the Princess had at last found paradise with the man she loved. The good fortune appeared boundless when the couple were able to return to a delightful new home at Kensington Palace, specially chosen by the Queen who remembered the house as her sister's favourite.

Though all was well in the immediate family, it was not so in the family of nations. The 'wind of change' which Macmillan had noted blowing through Africa was claiming its casualties. On 21 March, 1960 86 blacks were killed by police and 170 wounded in the Sharpeville Massacre, creating so much distaste at the policies of apartheid that a declaration of multi-racialism was made at the Commonwealth Conference at Windsor. Within the year a majority of white South Africans had voted to abolish the monarchy and the following year South Africa was out of the Commonwealth altogether, having refused to abandon apartheid. It was a sad end to an association which had begun so promisingly when Elizabeth made her twenty-first birthday speech in a spirit of optimism.

The Queen acquired two interesting new distinctions in 1961. She became an aunt for the seventeenth time, with the birth of a son, Viscount Linley, to Princess Margaret and her recently ennobled husband, now Lord Snowdon. The other sixteen nephews and nieces were the offspring of Prince Philip's sisters and only seen from time to time, whereas the new child might prove a very real companion for Andrew. The Queen's other distinction was to be voted 'Third Most Admired Woman in the World' in an American poll which put her just after Eleanor Roosevelt and Jackie Kennedy. Certainly it was a year in which she did her best to earn the accolade, finding time in an always busy schedule to entertain the new President Kennedy, visit the amiable Pope John at the Vatican and undertake more exhausting tours, most notably in India and Ghana. The latter was a particularly brave venture for the country was ruled by a despotic president, Kwame Nkrumah, who had locked away most of his opposition and was the target of assassination attempts. In spite of a bomb explosion five days before her intended arrival, the Queen would not be deterred from going and expressed to Prime Minister Macmillan her annoyance at being treated like a woman. Writing in his diary Macmillan could not refrain from quoting the words of her illustrious namesake, 'She has indeed "the heart and stomach of a man".'

Her Indian visit was another triumph, though a less dangerous one, embracing both the magic of Mogul India, as embodied in the Taj Mahal, and the stark realities of overcrowded, industrial Ahmedabad. Camels in Union Jacks knelt before her at the Republic Day parades, where nothing but good feeling was expressed for the daughter of the last Emperor and the nephew of the last Viceroy.

Top In May 1961 the Queen became the first British monarch ever to be given an audience by the Pope. John XXIII granted the royal couple twenty-five minutes of his time.

Above For once the Taj Mahal, magical even on a fairly dull day, was not the centre of attraction for most eyes during the royal tour of India in February 1961.

Opposite In Nepal's capital Katmandu, as in India, the Queen and her husband experienced the novelty of riding on elephant back. The animals are splendidly decked out in theur ceremonial attire and the Queen has been given a sunshade to protect her fair complexion.

Above, left **English weather contrasted badly with that enjoyed during the royal couple's visit to the Indian subcontinent. They were well wrapped against the elements for this visit to the 1961 Badminton Horse Trials with Prince Charles and Princess Margaret.**

Above **In off-duty moments the Queen favours headscarves as opposed to the fancy hats and glittering tiaras demanded for formal occasions. Here she is visiting what looks like a sale of handicrafts tent during the Royal Family's visit to the 1961 Badminton Horse Trials.**

Opposite, top Ascot in June is a 'must' for all the Royal Family. Early birds at the course might be lucky enough to witness the Queen galloping down the track hours before the official royal procession makes its way from nearby Windsor Castle at the start of the day's racing. This unusual photograph of the Queen was taken in 1961.

Top, left Always an admirer of equestrian excellence, the Queen rewards a competitor at the Royal Windsor Horse Show in May 1962. The event is held annually in the Home Park Public on the northern side of Windsor Castle and the Queen and other members of the Royal Family attend quite regularly.

Top, right This charmingly informal picture of mother and son was taken in August 1962 when Prince Andrew was two years old.

Left While at Balmoral for their 1961 holiday the Royal Family paid their customary visit to the nearby Braemar Highland Gathering. For the occasion the Queen sported a rather jaunty hat while Prince Philip donned his kilt.

The tour of India caused some controversy at home because in Jaipur it included a tiger hunt. Virtually every member of the Royal Family has at one time or another been criticised for their participation in blood sports. Prince Philip has linked his activities with those of conservation, while the Queen has tended to channel her animal and sporting interests into racing. She is generally acknowledged to be a very fine judge of a horse, with a great interest in each individually. Since her first successes in the 1940s with steeplechaser Monaveen, owned jointly with her mother, she has never looked back, though she decided to stick to flat racing when Monaveen was killed at a water-jump. It was a disappointment to lose the Coronation year Derby when her horse Aureole was beaten by Gordon Richards on Pinza, but 1954 made up for it when the horse won, amongst other races, the King George VI and Queen Elizabeth Stakes, to make the Queen leading winner-owner of the year.

Opposite, top The West African tour in November 1961 included a visit to Monrovia, the capital of Liberia, where the royal couple received an enthusiastic reception and the Union Jacks were out in force.

Opposite, bottom In spite of their many visits abroad in 1961 – to Cyprus, India, Pakistan, Nepal, Iran, Turkey, Italy and West Africa – the Queen and Prince Philip still managed to visit many parts of the British Isles, including Ulster. These happy waves of farewell were for Manchester as they left aboard the Royal Train.

Right A younger guard of honour than usual for the Queen as she attends the 1962 Gang Show at the Golders Green Empire on 28 November. These revues, with songs specially written by Ralph Reader, were a very popular item in the Boy Scout calendar.

Below A line-up of troops in Sierra Leone in 1961, the year the country gained its independence, during a royal visit to West Africa.

There has been a certain amount of criticism even of this activity, from those who feel the Queen should set an example by taking up more intellectual pursuits and devoting more time to the arts. In fact Her Majesty owns what is probably the finest private art collection in the world and is extremely knowledgeable about it. She also adds to it, the works of Graham Sutherland, Paul Nash and Alan Davie being among her acquisitions. Feeling that these treasures should be shared with as many others as possible, on 18 July 1962 she opened the Queen's Gallery to the public. Rebuilt on part of the bombed Buckingham Palace Chapel site, the gallery welcomed over 200,000 visitors to its first exhibition, 'Treasures from the Royal Collection'.

Appropriately enough the title of the following year's exhibition was 'Royal Children', for their ranks had been swelled in 1962 by the arrival of yet another boy, the Earl of St Andrews, a year after his parents, the Duke and Duchess of Kent, had married at York Minister with Princess Anne again a bridesmaid. The Kents soon had another addition to the family for on 24 April 1963 the Duke's sister Alexandra, one of the most popular of the royal ladies, married the Hon. Angus Ogilvy in Westminster Abbey.

With one thousand six hundred guests, including sixty European royals, the wedding was a splendid affair, preceded by an equally splendid banquet and ball given by the Queen in celebration. An extra entertainment provided the illustrious personages with the novel experience of being taken on a conducted tour of Windsor and its environs in two hired coaches with commentary courtesy of the Duke of Edinburgh and lunch at a pub on the Thames.

Left The scene in Westminster Abbey on 24 April 1963 as Princess Alexandra, the Queen's cousin, weds the Hon. Angus Ogilvy. Princess Anne was a bridesmaid and the distinguished guests included, besides the Queen herself, sixty members of European royal families.

Below July 1963 saw the state visit to Britain of King Paul and Queen Frederika of the Hellenes, who returned the Queen's hospitality by arranging a banquet for her at Claridge's Hotel, where she is seen arriving in one of her glamorous slim-line evening dresses.

Opposite, top As a farmer herself, with 5,000 acres of land around Sandringham, Windsor and Balmoral under cultivation, the Queen has more than an academic interest in agricultural shows. Here she is admiring some prize-winning sheep during a visit to the Royal Show held at Stoneleigh Abbey in Warwickshire in July 1963.

Opposite, bottom The Queen leaves Covent Garden Opera House in the company of King Baudouin of Belgium and the Earl of Home during the King's state visit to Britain in May 1963.

If it was 'welcome' to a new relation, it was also sadly the time to say 'farewell' to 'my guide and supporter through the mazes of international affairs and my instructor in many vital matters'. The feeling was assuredly mutual as Prime Minister Macmillan, stricken by illness, felt himself forced to resign after nearly seven years in office. As a mark of her affection the Queen came in person to his bedside at the King Edward VII hospital to sound out his views on who should be appointed as his successor. It was almost certainly Macmillan's advice that the candidacy of the Earl of Home triumphed. His days of power, and the amiable weekly briefing meetings with his monarch, were to be shortlived however, for in October 1964 he lost the election to Harold Wilson. It was to be the beginning of a new political era.

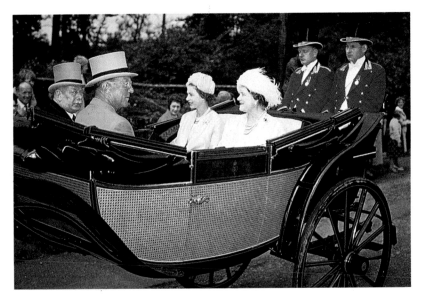

Left At the Royal Ascot meeting in 1963 the Queen accompanied her mother for the drive down the course before the opening race. They are sitting in one of the five Ascot landaus with their distinctive basket-work sides. Nearest the camera is the Duke of Beaufort who had been Master of the Horse in the Royal Household since 1936. Next to him is the Queen's uncle, the Duke of Gloucester.

Below A sunny day for 1963's Trooping the Colour ceremony as the Queen looks out over Horse Guards Parade from the back of her white horse. She rides side-saddle and wears the scarlet uniform of Colonel-in-Chief of the Household Brigade.

STRENGTHENING BONDS

Prince Edward, born on 10 March 1964, made a very early public appearance. After the Trooping the Colour ceremony in June his mother brought him out on to the balcony of Buckingham Palace to allow the crowds a brief glimpse. Prince Andrew seems to know what is required of him.

There was a decided air of expectancy around at the 1963 Christmas family get-together, last of its kind to be held at Sandringham. No less than four of the royal ladies present were looking forward to new arrivals in the spring. Princess Alexandra's son, James Ogilvy, put in his appearance first, managing like his mother, born on Christmas Day, to have an impossible birthday – 29 February. Then it was the Queen's turn to complete her 'second family' with the arrival on 10 March 1964 of a third son, Prince Edward, who was to be christened the day after Princess Margaret's daughter Lady Sarah Armstrong-Jones was born. He was given the names Edward Antony Richard Louis at a christening service which was the first royal one in a long time to have been held at Windsor Castle's private chapel. One of his godmothers, the Duchess of Kent, was unable to be present, having only four days earlier given birth to Lady Helen Windsor.

This year of new babies was also a year of new men at the top. With the advent of the first Labour government of the reign, headed by Harold Wilson, adjustments were to be required of both Queen and country. For the first time the Queen had a Prime Minister who was not public-school educated and who was from a decidedly lower class than the previous one (Sir Alec Douglas-Home's family was on friendly terms with the Queen's Scottish relations). Apparently they got on very well, Mr Wilson being quite devoted to her and she being anxious to benefit in particular from his knowledge of the lives of ordinary people in the industrial north.

Opposite The Sovereign of the Order of the Bath poses in her robes with other dignitaries after a service at the Order's Chapel in Westminster Abbey in October 1964. Amongst famous Knights of the Order have been Lord Nelson, the Duke of Wellington, Viscount Montgomery and Earl Mountbatten.

Below What this corgi was doing at the World Book Fair remains a mystery, but he could be sure of some royal attention when the Queen and Prince Philip arrived at Earl's Court to set the proceedings in motion on 10 June 1964.

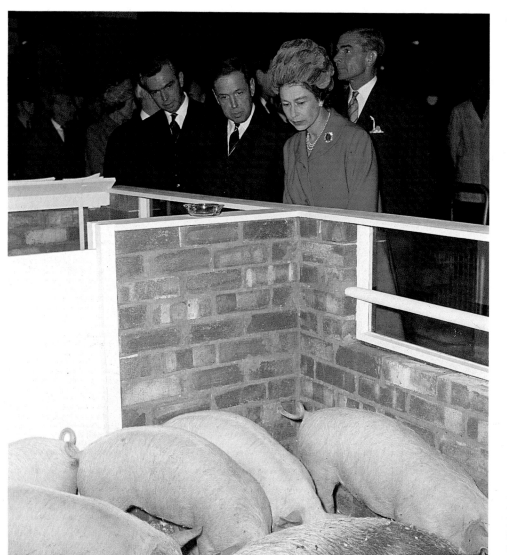

Left With the eye of an experienced farmer the Queen weighs up the potential of these porcine exhibits at 1964's Dairy Show at Olympia.

Opposite Another royal get-together at the Braemar Highland Gathering, this time in September 1964. Princess Margaret and Lord Snowdon share the rapt attention of three generations of royal ladies and a kilted Prince Charles.

Below In October 1964 there was a brief royal visit to Canada, during which the Queen was pleased to receive a bouquet from this young Brownie who must have reminded the Queen of her own Guiding days. There was so much opposition to the visit from French Canadians in Quebec that it was not an altogether happy experience for the royal couple.

Two of the Queen's major official visits of the year were to the north, though beyond Harold Wilson country and before he took up office. There was a week-long visit to Scotland in June, then she was back again in September to open the new Forth Bridge – for the 'unveiling' of a magnificent engineering achievement only the Queen's presence would suffice. Two years later it was to be the Severn Bridge that was so honoured.

The only overseas visit in 1964 was to Canada, bravely undertaken in view of the fact that President Kennedy had been assassinated less than a year earlier and there were threats against the Queen's life from French separatists. On 3 September, the *Daily Mirror* had blazoned across it the headline: 'We'll kill her on royal tour says Canadian killer gang'. Security had in the circumstances to be very tight, most especially in Quebec which was more like a city under siege than one in festive mood and where the Canadian police were particularly heavy-handed with their riot equipment. In the end the worst that befell the royal couple was to be greeted by small booing groups waving 'Go home' banners. It was still not the happiest of tours, perhaps explaining why the Queen's next visit, in 1967 on the centenary of Canada's confederation, was of less than a week's duration.

Above The Canadian Mounties were in splendid evidence during the Queen's visit to Canada in October 1964. Threats had been made against her life by French separatists so she needed their protection, but in the capital Ottawa there was a warm welcome.

Opposite In May 1965 it was felt that the Second World War had been over long enough to allow a state visit to West Germany. Here the Queen and her husband are chatting happily with President Lübke and his wife after a dinner party given for them in Bonn.

She had not been back four months when the Queen was saddened to learn of the death, on 24 January 1965, of her first Prime Minister. Having grown up during the war and close to the heart of decision-making, and having stood next to Winston Churchill on the Palace balcony that jubilant V-E Day, she fully understood the inspiration he had given. He in his turn had been half in love with his young monarch, keeping her picture by his bedside till the last. For an exceptional leader, there had to be an exceptional funeral. Departing entirely from the tradition that state funerals are only accorded to monarchs, the Queen ordered that this honour be given to Churchill. Five monarchs, six heads of state and sixteen prime ministers came to London to honour his memory, while thousands of the ordinary people to whom he had meant so much lined the streets to pay their last respects and millions of others watched on television. The Queen left the places of honour in St Paul's to commoners, allowing the Churchill family to enter after her, a gesture echoed on 1 November 1973 when she insisted that Lady Churchill and not she should unveil the statue of her husband in Parliament Square.

Opposite, top The Queen had been fond of circuses ever since she was taken to her first one in early childhood. Even as an adult her pleasure at meeting Coco the Clown during a visit to Bertram Mills Circus in 1965 seems very genuine.

Below This charming springtime snapshot was taken in the Home Park at Windsor Castle just before the Queen's thirty-ninth birthday on 21 April 1965. In the background is Frogmore House, once the home of Queen Charlotte, wife of George III.

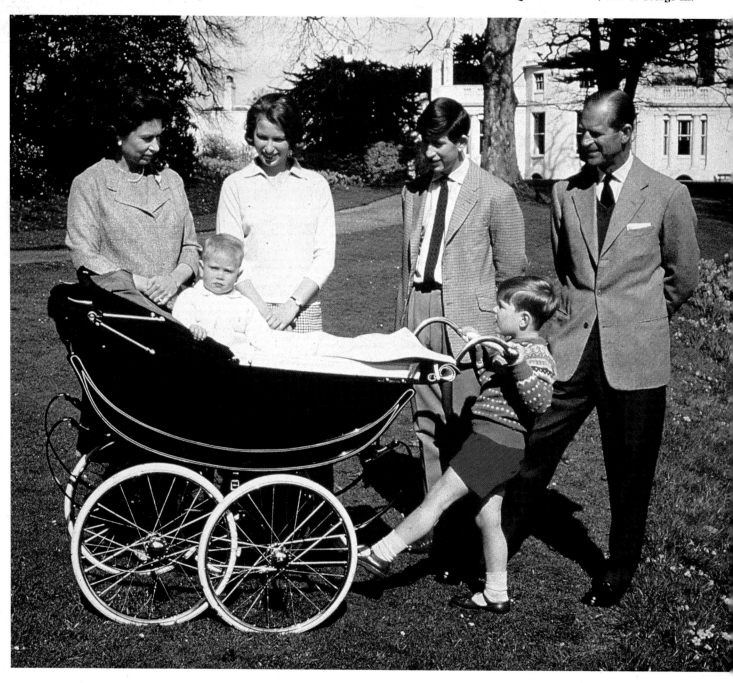

Left **Earl Mountbatten of Burma welcomes his sovereign to Carisbrooke Castle in 1965 to preside at his installation as Governor of the Isle of Wight. Typically, he organised the ceremony himself and even arranged for the castle's main gate to be removed for the first time in 300 years to allow the royal car through.**

Another sadness was the death of the Princess Royal, the Queen's aunt, just over a month later, but if it was a year of sad farewells it was also one of happy family reunions. Prince Philip's three surviving older sisters had always maintained a very low profile while visiting their relatives in Britain. They were all married to Germans and so soon after the war it had not been thought diplomatic to advertise the Queen's German connections. They had not therefore been invited to their brother's wedding back in 1947 and although Prince Philip had from the first made private unpublicised visits to them in Germany and later taken his children, his wife had never accompanied him.

Now, twenty years after the war, it seemed as if nations governed by new generations might be able to heal old wounds, and the Queen was invited to make a state visit to West Germany. While there she felt able to refer to her own German origins, her direct descent from the Elector of Hanover who became George I, but she was uncomfortable with the almost hysterical reception given to her by the massive crowds, especially in Berlin. It was a relief to escape on her 'days off' to those homes of the in-laws in Salem and Langenburg which she had only ever seen in photographs before and to be reunited with some of the myriad of German relatives.

The education of the Queen's eldest son was meanwhile taking some unusual, if not extraordinary, turns. While at Cheam, Prince Charles received what was undoubtedly highly prejudiced paternal

Opposite The royal couple enjoying a jolly evening out at the Royal Company of Archers' Ball in Edinburgh in 1966.

Below There was a royal tour of the Caribbean in February 1966. In Barbados the Queen visited the College of Arts and Science, where she received this bouquet.

Above A one-day visit was made to Belfast on 4 July 1966 so that the Queen could open the bridge named after her. Later in the year she was called on to open an even more spectacular engineering achievement, the 5240-foot-long Severn Bridge.

Right During a visit to the Filton Works in Bristol in September 1966 the Queen was shown this model of supersonic airliner Concorde. The technological miracle achieved by British and French engineers was not to become a reality until more than two years later.

advice about where he should go next. 'I freely subjected myself to what he thought best, because I had perfect confidence in my father's judgment.' And so it was that Prince Charles found himself being flown up to Gordonstoun by his father in the summer of 1962. The Queen had already vetted her son's home for the next three and a half years and was somewhat appalled by its austerity. Nevertheless he was to survive the regime of early-morning cold showers and do-it-yourself housework, creating press sensations only twice – once when he innocently ordered a cherry brandy when under-age in a Stornoway bar during a school cruise, and again when pages of his exercise book (containing nothing extraordinary) were stolen and sold for publication to the German magazine *Stern*.

It would not be fair to say that these were the happiest days of Charles's life, but he really did enjoy himself when he was sent to Geelong Grammar School in Australia at the beginning of 1966 to get to know one small part of the Commonwealth's largest island really well. He hated leaving Britain, but in the end was to declare that 'Australia conquered my shyness'. Far away from the great Australian cities with their publicity-seekers, he was treated as just another 'pommy' by boys to whom the English aristocracy meant nothing and who judged people by how they found them. In the end Charles had to drag himself back to Gordonstoun to obtain the two A-levels which were to gain him entry to Trinity College, Cambridge, in 1967.

Princess Anne, too, was departing from the usual tradition of royal education. For a while she had lessons from a governess at the Palace in the company of two other girls specially brought in from outside. Then, at the age of thirteen, she was sent away to Benenden, a girls' boarding school in Kent. Anxious to see her settled in happily, the Queen broke her holiday at Balmoral so that she could deliver her daughter personally into the care of the

Top, middle **Another annual event for the Royal Family is morning service at St George's Chapel, Windsor, on Christmas Day. Here they are seen leaving after the 1967 service.**

Above **Tragedy at Aberfan. The Queen and the Duke of Edinburgh were quick to offer their sympathy to grieving parents at the Welsh mining village where in October 1966 a slag tip collapsed on to a school and a row of houses killing 144 people, including 116 children.**

headmistress. While at Benenden the Princess kept up the riding lessons which had commenced soon after the Queen first put reins into her two-year-old hands and which were to set her on the road to a personal achievement which owed little to status and a great deal to courage, determination and skill.

The next few years for the Queen continued to follow the by now well-established pattern, with a visit or two abroad each year and many, many visits around the country. She was at Aberfan in October 1966 to commiserate with grieving relatives and talk with rescue workers only days after the awful disaster in which a slag tip collapsed on to a school, nearly wiping out one generation of a Welsh village. She also attended happier events such as the launching of the liner *Queen Elizabeth II* at Clydebank on 20 September 1967 and the opening of the Tyne Tunnel.

Right During her tour of Brazil and Chile in November 1968 the Queen was persuaded to pose on the tarmac of Santiago airport with her RAF personnel. On the far right is the Commander of the Queen's Flight, Air Commodore Archie Winskill.

Below, right The Queen looks particularly stunning in the rich blue and red Mantle of the Order of St Michael and St George. She was attending one of the Order's services at St Paul's Cathedral in 1968.

Below, left An annual event for the Queen is the State Opening of Parliament in November, here in 1967. Her two eldest children were present for the first time.

At the Palace a steady stream of visiting heads of state and other celebrities continued to be received. Among the distinguished, and not so distinguished, Americans so honoured in 1969 were the Apollo 11 crew – which included the first man to walk on the moon, and President Nixon, blissfully unaware that his bubble was one day going to burst.

President Nixon arrived in time to make a 'guest appearance' in the film *Royal Family*, shown on television in 1969. Two earlier productions, one on royal palaces, the other a celluloid biography of Lord Mountbatten, had paved the way and their success had persuaded the Queen that giving the people some idea of her life and work would bring her closer to them and create greater understanding. The BBC film crew was allowed to film whatever it pleased, though the Queen had veto of the footage finally used, and in all she gave some seventy-five days of her time for the shooting. She was shown in various of her homes, entertaining important dignitaries or relaxing with the family. On the whole it was viewed with rapt attention, going on to become the world's most popular documentary ever.

Below **President Nixon arrived for lunch at Buckingham Palace on 25 February 1969 and found himself with a bit part in the film** *Royal Family.* **Made jointly by the BBC and Independent Television, it had its first television showing on 21 June and was an enormous success.**

Opposite, bottom **The film** *Royal Family* **was an eye-opener for the Queen's subjects, who were treated to scenes never filmed before, here an after-lunch discussion.**

Above, right **This BBC cameraman had to be up early to record the Queen and her trainer watching the royal horses try out their paces on the Berkshire Downs.**

Below A bonfire at Sandringham in June 1969.

Bottom Frogmore in spring on the Queen's forty-second birthday in 1968.

Opposite On 19 May 1969 the Queen opened the General Assembly of the Church of Scotland, the first time since the Reformation that a reigning monarch had done so.

The Royal Family provided another television spectacular in July of that year when they took part in the greatest ceremonial occasion since the Coronation. The Queen was fulfilling her earlier promise to present her son to the people of Wales. He had already decided to get to know the principality better by enrolling for a term at Aberystwyth earlier in the year and had mastered enough of the Welsh language to delight the huge Investiture gathering at Caernarvon with a short speech in their own tongue. In a setting designed by Lord Snowdon and dressed in picturesque robes, the Prince knelt before his mother in the middle of the huge medieval amphitheatre of the castle to receive from her his crown and to promise, in words reminiscent of his father's at the Coronation, to 'become your liege man of life and limb and of earthly worship'. After the ceremony mother and son appeared on the battlements of the castle, where the Prince could truly be presented to the people and where joy was apparent on all sides.

Opposite A proud mother presents her son to the people of Wales at the Queen's Gate of Caernarvon Castle on 1 July 1969. He wears the uniform of the Royal Regiment of Wales, together with the insignia of his office – the coronet, ring, rod, sword and ceremonial mantle of ermine-furred crimson velvet.

Above One of the supreme moments of 1969's big event. Having crowned her son the twenty-first Prince of Wales in the historic setting of Caernarvon Castle, the Queen receives his homage. Prince Charles's magnificent gold coronet was specially designed for him and presented by the Goldsmiths' Company.

Left After the Prince of Wales's Investiture he received a Loyal Address from the People of Wales, which he replied to partly in Welsh, to the delight of the four thousand invited guests. Then he and his mother walked in procession from the royal dais to the Queen's Gate for the presentation to the people.

All in all 1969 was a good year in which to be royal and to celebrate your twenty-first birthday, as Charles did in November. The event was marred only by the obvious decline in the health of his paternal grandmother, Princess Andrew, now a fellow-resident at the Palace, but she did live long enough to enjoy both the royal film and the Investiture before she died in December.

Other members of the family received a fair amount of media attention around this time, though the two younger Princes were allowed to pursue their educational studies with much less harassment than had attended Prince Charles. In fact the Queen had really been able to enjoy the growing-up of her youngest sons, spending far more time with them than she had ever felt able to give her two older children.

Above **The Queen was one of the very first passengers to try out a new stretch of the Victoria line in March 1969 and first monarch to sample the London Underground.**

Above, left **Essential headgear during the Queen's visit to the Basic Oxygen steelmaking plant at Port Talbot in 1970.**

Top **Princess Anne was able to join her parents on their state visit to Austria in May 1969. This photograph was taken with the Austrian President and his wife.**

Below In their youth both the Queen and Princess Margaret derived enormous pleasure from their Guide and Brownie activities. They were pleased, therefore, to join with Lady Baden-Powell in celebrating the Diamond Jubilee of the Girl Guides Association at the Banqueting Hall in Whitehall in 1970.

Below President Nixon and his wife made the briefest of visits to Britain in October 1970 and the Queen did them the honour of driving down to

Chequers, the Prime Minister's country home, to have lunch with them and Edward Heath.

Above The Queen and Prince Philip photographed with their two older children at Sandringham in 1970.

Mini-skirted Princess Anne was now proving very news-worthy, not least for American pressmen when she accompanied her brother on a visit to the Nixons in the White House in 1970. Having left school, she was caught up in the royal round of duties and was living up to her tomboyish image by, amongst other things, visiting a North Sea gas rig complete with safety helmet and overalls, driving a fifty-two-ton tank and being stopped twice by the police for speeding. Relations with the press, many of whom thought her rude and uncooperative, were improved considerably when in 1971, the year of her twenty-first birthday, she won the European Horse Trials and was voted Sportswoman of the Year. For a mother so utterly devoted to horses it must have been a proud moment indeed as the Queen stepped out to present the Raleigh Trophy to her daugher, the Individual Three-Day Event Winner, at Burghley in September.

Though her children were beginning to steal some of the limelight there was one important innovation at this time which attracted a lot of attention and served to bring the monarch closer to the people, and that was the introduction of the 'walkabout'. The first experiments were during the 1970 visit to New Zealand, delightfully detached from so much of the violence elsewhere in the world and a most loyally royalist part of the Commonwealth. Stopping to chat to faces picked at random out of the crowd or to accept a small child's posy, the Queen no longer seemed so remote and cold, and first events of the kind proved so successful that there was no leaving them out of future tours or denying them to inhabitants of the home country.

Left The north of England welcomed the Queen with warm weather on the October day in 1971 when she came to open Scammonden Water by the M62 motorway.

Opposite, bottom The Queen was out on horseback in Windsor Great Park in May 1971 to watch a coaching marathon but stopped for a chat with Lord Westmorland and Mrs Joan Wills, lady in waiting to Princess Margaret.

Above These schoolboys follow in a distinguished tradition which was four hundred years old in 1971. The Queen joined them at Harrow to celebrate the school's foundation.

Below The Queen was quite taken aback to be greeted by Mr Tod the Fox when she arrived for a film premiere, but perhaps she should not have been for the film was MGM's *Tales of Beatrix Potter*, a charming interpretation by ballet dancers of the famous animal stories.

Opposite, top King Taufa'ahau Tupou IV welcomes the Queen and Prince Philip and their daughter to a Royal Feast in Tonga in March 1970 during their Australasian tour. Back in 1953 the King's mother Queen Salote had been one of the stars of the Coronation and had later given the royal couple a warm welcome when they visited her home.

Opposite, bottom The state visit of Queen Juliana and Prince Bernhard of the Netherlands in April 1972 was a glittering affair, with a magnificent banquet at Windsor Castle in honour of the Dutch monarch. The royal ladies were also present en masse for this evening function at Carpenters' Hall in the City.

Right, bottom It is often a decided advantage to be royal. Thousands of Londoners queued for hours to see the Treasures of Tutankhamum exhibition at the British Museum in 1972 whereas the Queen got in quite easily and on the first day. She did have to declare it open and endure the mass of waiting photographers, however.

Below However great the star, the Queen is always the leading lady. Here it is Barbra Streisand meeting an appreciative member of the audience at the 1975 royal première of her film *Funny Lady*. Co-star James Cann awaits his turn.

Below Delightful Queen Sirikit was hostess to the Queen and Princess Anne during their visit to Thailand with the Duke of Edinburgh in 1972. It must have been a relief to exchange the umbrellas of an English February for these oriental sunshades.

If the Queen was trying to cement ties within the Commonwealth, there were events happening in Britain which seemed to be threatening its very existence. In January 1972 Prime Minister Heath signed the Treaty of Accession which would take Britain into the European Economic Community the following year and there were many voices of foreboding. The Queen must have had very ambivalent feelings. She had strong family ties with several European countries. At the same time she was passionately devoted to the Commonwealth and had probably travelled to more parts of it and met more of its inhabitants than anyone else alive. It seemed hardly an accident that in the very year of EEC entry she was flying out to Ottawa, invited extraordinarily enough by Pierre Trudeau, a French-Canadian Prime Minister with hitherto republican leanings, to attend her first Commonwealth Conference outside London. It seemed as if she was emphasising the renewed importance of the Crown's unifying role as the Head of the Commonwealth at a time when the mother country itself was acquiring a new allegiance.

Neither a family of nations nor an ordinary human one remains static and the Queen's cousins, the Kents and the Ogilvys, were continuing to add to theirs. In 1966 Princess Alexandra gave birth to a daughter, Marina, named after the Princess's universally

Below In June 1967 the Duke and Duchess of Windsor were in London to attend the unveiling by the Queen of a plaque in the wall of Marlborough House commemorating the hundredth anniversary of Queen Mary's birth. It was their first official visit to England.

loved Greek mother who was sadly to die only two years after this event and never to know the grandson Nicholas born in 1970.

There were still, alas, skeletons in the family cupboard. Edward VIII after his abdication had been made Duke of Windsor and gone into voluntary exile in Paris with his American wife, who to his chagrin continued to be denied the title 'Royal Highness'. During a stay at the London Clinic for eye surgery in March 1965 he found his bedside visited by the Queen, first of several members of the Royal Family to make this conciliatory gesture. It was not an example which the Queen Mother could follow, still unable to forget those days of 1936 which had so utterly transformed her own life and the lives of her husband and daughters. The Windsors were actually invited to London in 1967 to be present at the unveiling of a memorial to the Duke's mother, Queen Mary. After he died at his Paris home on 28 May 1972 the Queen was able to telegraph her condolences to the widow and end by expressing her gladness 'that I was able to see him in Paris ten days ago'. She had taken time off during a state visit to do so. At the funeral at St George's Chapel, Windsor, the widow was at last accorded the respect her husband had always sought for her when she was seated between the Queen and Prince Philip, her hosts at Buckingham Palace. The one-time King was laid to rest at Frogmore, near Windsor Castle.

155

Below **The Duke of Windsor died at his Paris home on 28 May 1972, only days after his favourite niece had visited him there. At his funeral at St George's Chapel, Windsor, his widow sat next to the Queen and the Duke, her hosts at Buckingham Palace.**

There was another, and tragically unexpected, death later in the year. Prince William of Gloucester, who was confidently expected to succeed his father as Duke, was killed when the plane he was piloting during an air race crashed. Only months earlier he had been best man at the wedding of his brother Richard to Birgitte van Deurs, daughter of a Danish lawyer. Prince Richard, who had been quietly carving out a career for himself as an architect, instead found himself inheriting the family estates and title when his father died in 1974, shortly before the birth of their first child, the Earl of Ulster.

Opposite While on board *Britannia* Lord Lichfield was subjected to the indignities meted out to those making a sea crossing of the equator for the first time. He was covered with shaving soap and ducked in a pool several times but, ever-vigilant photographer that he is, kept a waterproof camera at the ready and managed to capture this delightfully spontaneous shot of the Queen laughing at his discomfiture.

Left Even for the much-travelled monarch this buggy seems a somewhat unconventional mode of transport but she and the Duke are obviously enjoying every minute in the company of President Tito of Yugoslavia and his wife. They were all visiting the island of Vanga in October 1972 during the Queen's first state visit to a communist country.

Below Lord Lichfield was invited to photograph his royal cousin on her visit to South-East Asia and the Indian Ocean in February and March 1972, and this is his delightful picture of the Queen with President Kenyatta and his wife at a tribal display in Nairobi.

Above **Waving to the crowds who had come out to wish her joy on this day of celebration. At a Guildhall luncheon after the Silver Wedding service of thanksgiving the Queen declared: 'If I am asked what I think about family life, I am for it.'**

Opposite **Another memento of Lord Lichfield's Balmoral visit. The Queen looks truly at home with her corgis in this idyllic setting. Knowing the extensive grounds intimately, the Queen herself was able to suggest this waterfall as a background, a choice which also proved popular with thousands of postcard-buyers.**

Right **Silver Wedding Day itself. Looking elegant in a mink-trimmed ice-blue silk coat worn with a matching hat of cascading ostrich feathers, the Queen walks in procession with her husband down the aisle of Westminster Abbey after the service of thanksgiving commemorating their marriage there on 20 November 1947.**

Page 158–159 **The Queen and Prince Philip raise Highland cattle on the Balmoral estate.**

Page 159, inset **Lord Lichfield was lucky enough to be a guest at Balmoral in the summer of 1971 and to enjoy a ride through the grounds in the company of his hostess. It was a working holiday, however, and one of its products was this fascinating picture taken specially for her Silver Wedding year of the Queen surveying her Highland estate.**

The year was not all sorrow. Towards the end came the Queen and the Duke's Silver Wedding anniversary. A hundred other similarly celebrating couples were invited to the service of thanksgiving in Westminster Abbey, happy scene of their first union those many years ago. Then there was a luncheon at the Guildhall at which the Queen brought smiles to all faces when she rose to say: 'I think everyone will concede that today, of all occasions, I should begin my speech with "My husband and I".' She went on to give unequivocal praise to the married condition and to declare: 'If I am asked what I think about family life, I am for it.' For an hour afterwards the Queen and her husband and their two eldest children went on an unprecedented walkabout in the streets of the City where they were greeted with great affection by multitudes of ordinary people, happy to share in the joy of the occasion. That evening there was a private party at the Palace, sprung on the Queen and the Duke as a surprise by Prince Charles and Princess Anne, who had invited every one of their parents' friends from the last twenty-five years that they could think of. The two younger brothers were home from their school, Heatherdown, for the occasion, and the guest list included, at Princess Anne's insistence, a certain Lieutenant Phillips whom the rest of the family were soon to get to know rather well!

This photograph was specially taken by Patrick Lichfield to commemorate the Queen and Prince Philip's Silver Wedding. He had to seize the opportunity of nearly all the Royal Family being together at Windsor Castle on Boxing Day 1971 and then had to stand on a ladder to get them all in.

Princess Anne had met Mark Phillips, then training for a career in the Army at the Royal Military College, Sandhurst, through their mutual love of horses. On horseback Lieutenant Phillips, though a commoner, was very much the equal of his royal rival and in 1972 he, and not she, had been chosen to represent Britain at the Munich Olympics, though the Princess had flown out to watch him win his Olympic Gold Medal. As soon as the Press had wind of what might be going on, they of course did their best to make the couple's lives a misery. It was something of a relief when, on 29 May 1973, the engagement was at last announced. It was to the Duke of Edinburgh and not the Queen that the 'petrified' Mark had had to make his request for their daughter's hand. The pair were so obviously in love and ruled by the same equine passion that the royal parents thought them ideally suited in spite of the Lieutenant's lack of royal pedigree.

Below, left A fine judge of a horse, the Queen weighs up the quality of the runners in the enclosure at Epsom on Derby Day, 1973. Her skill speaks for itself in the number of winners she has owned over the years, though her horses have consistently failed to win the Derby.

Below, right A happy day for two families. Princess Anne's parents pose with Mr and Mrs Phillips on either side of a young couple newly engaged and obviously very much in love. The date was 30 May 1973, and within six months the Queen's daughter would be married to a commoner.

Above, left The Queen chats happily to a member of her ceremonial bodyguard, the Royal Company of Archers, during a garden party in the grounds of the Palace of Holyroodhouse in Edinburgh in July 1973. She usually spends about a week of the year here.

Above right The Patron of the Royal College of Music looks delighted at having the opportunity to present to her mother the honorary degree of Doctor of Music. The ceremony was held on 5 December 1973.

It was on 14 November, 1973, her older brother's twenty-fifth birthday, that the royal Princess, while keeping her title, became plain Mrs Mark Phillips. She made an elegant bride as she went up the aisle of Westminster Abbey on her father's arm before the eyes of twenty-five royal guests and hundreds of others in the Abbey itself and of course millions of television viewers. Much of the couple's honeymoon was spent in the seclusion of the royal yacht, though they managed quick visits to South America and the West Indies before flying back to join the rest of the family at Windsor for Christmas. Captain Phillips had the opportunity to learn at first hand from the professionalism of his in-laws when the couple joined the Queen and the Duke and Prince Charles on their Australasian tour early in the following year.

Bottom **Visits from Scandinavian royalty are always happy occasions and that by Queen Margrethe and Prince Henrik of Denmark in May 1974 was no exception.**

Opposite **The new Mrs Mark Phillips and her husband acknowledge the good wishes of the crowd.**

Below, left **The Queen was at Sandhurst on 30 May 1974 to present new colours to the Royal Military Academy. By this time her daughter and son-in-law were resident at Oak Grove House in the grounds of Sandhurst.**

Below, right **Captain Phillips had his first experience of a Commonwealth tour early on in his royal career. As the Queen's personal aide-de-camp, he was attending the opening of Parliament in Wellington, New Zealand, with his wife.**

The Queen was on yet another overseas visit, this time to Indonesia, when Princess Anne again hit the headlines, this time through no fault of her own. News was phoned through to the Queen that Anne and Mark while returning to Buckingham Palace from a charity film performance had been ambushed in the Mall. A gunman had seized the Princess and tried to drag her from her car, in the process wounding her chauffeur and bodyguard and a policeman and journalist who happened to be passing. Fortunately rescue was at hand, but the Princess had behaved with such cool courage throughout her ordeal that her mother felt proud to bestow on her the Royal Victorian Order.

Above The sun does not always shine, not even for royal garden parties, but nothing can stop those honoured with invitations from turning up to see the Queen and her family at home. This sea of umbrellas was keeping a little patch of Buckingham Palace's lawn dry during a wet July day in 1975.

Left May 1975 saw the first visit by a reigning sovereign to the colony of Hong Kong and the citizens were out in their boats to honour the Queen at a sail-past in one of the harbours. They called her their '*Lui Wong*' or 'Woman King'.

Below Not thinking about what to buy for Sunday lunch but wondering at the diversity of exotic vegetables on display at this stall in a Hong Kong street market during her 1975 visit to the colony. Though only there a few days, the royal couple managed to crowd a great variety of engagements into their tour.

Opposite Sporting the moustache which caused a minor press sensation, Prince Charles walks in procession along the nave of Westminster Abbey after the ceremony on 28 May 1975 during which his mother installed him as Great Master of the Order of the Bath.

Below A royal line-up at Holyroodhouse during the Swedish state visit to Scotland in July 1975. From left to right are the Duke of Gloucester, Princess Margaret, Prince Charles, the Queen, King Carl Gustav, Mr John Ambler, husband of Princess Margaretha of Sweden, the Queen Mother, Princess Margaretha and Prince Philip.

Interesting things were happening in politics at this time which were to affect the Queen directly. In 1975 Mrs Thatcher was the first woman to be elected leader of the Conservative Party and the Queen had the prospect of one day working with a female Prime Minister. Harold Wilson, with whom she had always got on so well, resigned in 1976, leaving her to form a new relationship with the avuncular James Callaghan. Before Wilson left office there had been a dramatic intervention by the Crown in Australian politics when on 11 November 1975 the Governor-General, an appointee of the Queen herself, dismissed the Labour Prime Minister, Gough Whitlam, and appointed the Liberal Malcolm Fraser as caretaker in his place. Though the unpopularity of the Government was shown when it lost the following election, and the action of the Governor-General appeared to have given expression to the general Australian feeling at the time, the issue raised some worrying questions about the power of the Crown.

Worrying questions had been asked for some time about the future of Princess Margaret and Lord Snowdon's marriage, more and more unhappy reports of which were making their way into the gossip columns. Unhappily, substance was given to the rumours when on 19 March 1976 a separation was announced. It was all very civilised, with the Princess retaining custody of the two children and the family home and Lord Snowdon being allowed unlimited access. Sad as she was that unhappiness still seemed to dog her sister's footsteps, the Queen continued on friendly terms with Lord Snowdon, who is still called to the Palace to take some of the finest of the official photographs. Both he and his estranged wife were guests at the party held only weeks after their separation to celebrate the Queen's fiftieth birthday. The excitement of 20 April began with a dinner for sixty at Windsor Castle. Another 500 guests joined the select few for a ball which followed in the evening and then at 2.40 a.m., the precise moment when fifty years ago she had

Below **Looking at her most informal but still the focal point of attention, the Queen gets involved in some earnest discussion with the Duke of Beaufort at 1976's Badminton Horse Trials. Sharing the grassy enclosure are Princess Margaret, her daughter Lady Sarah Armstrong-Jones and the Queen Mother.**

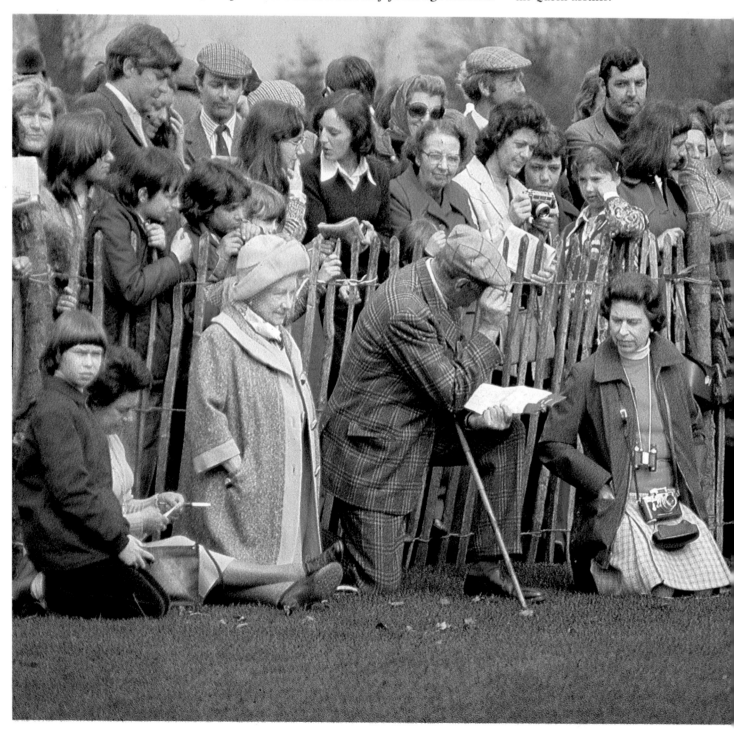

entered the world at No. 17 Bruton Street, the Queen was swept on to the dance floor by her husband to the strains of Joe Loss's band. A night indeed to remember.

The Montreal Olympics later in the year proved not quite as memorable for the British equestrian team as had been hoped. After a visit to the United States to share in the American Bicentennial celebrations the Queen went to Canada with the Duke to open the Games and to show particular interest in the progress of her daughter and son-in-law, the first husband and wife to be selected as part of the British team. In the event Mark Phillips was not actually chosen to ride and in the cross-country section the Princess had a nasty fall, though in the interests of her team she bravely insisted on finishing the course. It was all to no avail, but the Queen and the Duke could content themselves with their daughter's achievement in having taken part in the Games and done so in the true spirit of the Olympic ideal.

Below **All the family were in Canada in 1976 to see Princess Anne competing in the Montreal Olympics and to pose beside the lake at Bromont for this happy snapshot. The Queen opened the Games but was not lucky enough to witness a British triumph in the equestrian events.**

THE JUBILEE YEARS

It could almost have been a scene from the Coronation as the Queen and the Duke left Buckingham Palace in the Gold State Coach for the Silver Jubilee thanksgiving service at St Paul's Cathedral. Even the weather was reminiscent of June 1953 – dull and damp.

If in the past few years it had looked as if attention was being deflected from the Queen herself on to other members of the family, 1977 was assuredly the year when all this was reversed. There was of course plenty of advance information that this was to be Jubilee Year, but for a while it seemed as if it might be rather a low-key affair. The Queen herself in her 1976 Christmas broadcast appeared to support those who argued against extravagant celebrations at a time of economic hardship when she declared 'The gift I would most value next year is that reconciliation should be found wherever it is needed.' In the event the nation went wild as it had not done since Coronation year. There were flags and bunting and street parties the length of the land, in addition to the huge programme of official functions.

It was realised that in this year, above all others, millions would want to see the Queen and so she embarked early on her tours. At her grandfather George V's Jubilee, the Empire – in the form of its rulers – came to London. In the changed times of the 1970s the Queen must go out to meet and be seen by ordinary people and so on 10 February she embarked on a Commonwealth tour more extensive than any undertaken since that of 1953–54. Travelling by royal yacht, train, car and plane – even supersonic Concorde – she and the Duke covered 56,000 miles, giving particular pleasure to the crowds with that 1970s innovation of the walkabout.

Opposite, top One stop on the Royal Jubilee Tour of Australasia, which took place in February and March 1977 was Tonga, where the Queen and the Duke were invited to a banquet in a hut made from coconut and bamboo leaves. Their host King Taufa'ahau Tupou appreciates his food, as is suggested by his size in comparison with his wife and their guests.

Opposite, bottom The tour covered much the same ground as the Queen's Coronation Tour. Senior chiefs went out to meet the royal yacht when it arrived at Fiji and one of them presented the Queen with a whale's tooth.

Below The events of Silver Jubilee year got off to an early start. This was 8 February and the Queen was out planting a small oak tree in Victoria Tower Gardens beside the Palace of Westminster to inaugurate the tree-planting programme which was but one of the many schemes celebrating her twenty-five years on the throne.

The overseas tour was in two parts, the first ending in late March, the second taking place in the latter half of October. In between there was the whole of Britain to be covered, or as much as was reasonably possible. Concentrating on the areas of heaviest population, she was to visit thirty-six counties, the highlight of her northern visit being a ceremonial drive along Edinburgh's Royal Mile on 23 May. She bravely ended her British tour in August with a two-day trip to Northern Ireland, that most troubled part of the kingdom, where she was obliged to travel by royal yacht and helicopter amidst the strictest security, which nevertheless allowed her to meet a varied selection of her law-abiding subjects including the leaders of the Peace Movement.

Above **People at home as well as those in the Commonwealth wanted to see the monarch in her Jubilee year and Scotland got its turn in May when Glasgow witnessed this ceremonial drive to the City Chambers.**

Right In the Queen's Silver Jubilee year it was appropriate that if she was to review a parade of cars at Windsor Castle in May it should be one of Silver Ghost Rolls-Royces. Still the world's most prestigious car, the British-made Rolls has lost nothing by its royal patronage.

Below The world's most famous ballet partnership ever was to pay its own tribute to the Queen at a Silver Jubilee Gala on 30 May 1977. Dame Margot Fonteyn, still dancing in her fifties, curtseys before the royal guest whilst her Russian-born partner Rudolf Nureyev looks on.

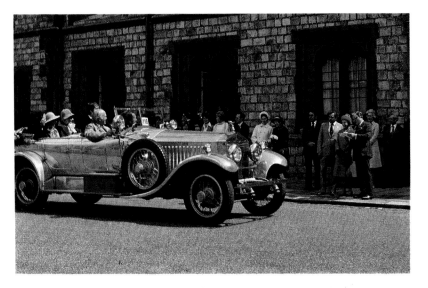

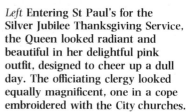

Left **Entering St Paul's for the Silver Jubilee Thanksgiving Service, the Queen looked radiant and beautiful in her delightful pink outfit, designed to cheer up a dull day. The officiating clergy looked equally magnificent, one in a cope embroidered with the City churches.**

Politicians as well as people had to pay their respects in this special year and on 4 May she was at Westminster Hall to receive a verbal tribute from Mr Callaghan and loyal addresses from the Lords and the Commons, both incidentally given by Welshman, Lord Elwyn-Jones and George Thomas. The Queen in reply praised the virtues of the nation she had been called to serve, 'the basic stability of our institutions, our traditions of public service and concern for others, our family life and, above all, the freedom you have through the ages so fearlessly upheld'.

Foreign leaders were also in Britain in this Jubilee year. In May the Queen gave a dinner party at the Palace for seven western ones, among them newly elected President Carter, President Giscard d'Estaing from across the Channel and old acquaintance Pierre Trudeau. The latter was to turn up again when the Queen entertained leaders attending the Commonwealth Conference in June.

The high point of the Jubilee festivities also came in June, with Jubilee Day itself on the seventh. Looking delightful in a festive pink outfit crowned with its own peal of celebratory bells, the Queen drove with her husband in the Gold State Coach, not used since the Coronation, to St Paul's. If she sometimes looked a little tired and strained during the Thanksgiving Service, this was dispelled as soon as she was out with the crowds on a walkabout to the Guildhall, where she was to lunch as guest of the City. London had never seen anything like it before. The Queen was indeed 'happy and glorious' and her people delighted to find her so. Masses of them crowded into the Mall later in the day to cheer madly as she waved joyfully from the Palace balcony, perhaps relieved that the strains of the last few hours were over, but certainly delighted at a day which had fulfilled her ideal of shared experience – the Queen and her family among, and at one with, the people.

Above In June South-East London had its chance to celebrate the Silver Jubilee with the Queen. Here she is on a walkabout in Deptford. Whenever possible she and the Duke left the royal car to stroll among the people, though the police were never far away.

Below From St Paul's the Queen walked with the Lord Mayor of London to the Guildhall for a luncheon in her honour, delighting these flag-waving wellwishers on the way. The peal of bells on her pink hat seemed to echo the festive spirit of London on this day.

Above The Queen replies to the loyal address by the Lord Mayor of London, Sir Robin Gillett, after the lunch given in her honour at the Guildhall on Jubilee Day. As well as being the Queen's own special day, it was also a family celebration.

The year was to see spectacular displays of fireworks, most notably that held on the Thames two days after Jubilee Day, and a nationwide chain of bonfires lit on the eve of Jubilee Day symbolising a nation united in its affection for Her Majesty. Since the Queen was head of the Armed Forces there had to be displays of power as well as affection. She went to Germany to review that part of the Army stationed there, but the Silver Jubilee Fleet Review was probably the most impressive event. At Spithead one hundred and eighty ships lined up for inspection by the Queen from her vantage-point on the Royal Yacht *Britannia*. There were craft of all types, not only from Britain and the Commonwealth, but also from European countries and from America.

As in another important year of her reign, 1969, a television film was made which only added to the Queen's lustre. Though the BBC's *Royal Heritage* purported to be 'the Story of Britain's Builders and Collectors', it was really about the Queen herself and her family. She was shown using items collected by her ancestors or giving guided tours round some of her priceless art treasures and historic homes.

Opposite Virginia Wade did Queen and country proud by winning the Wimbledon Women's Singles title at last, and in Jubilee year. It was also the centenary year of the championships and the Queen was there to present the overjoyed winner with her trophy.

Below Alongside the Queen as she acknowledged the waves of affection which on Jubilee Day were for her above all others were her husband and family and the man who had been a guide and friend to them throughout the reign, Lord Mountbatten.

Right As Admiral of the Fleet, Lord Mountbatten was again present when 180 ships from Britain, Europe, America and the Commonwealth assembled at Spithead for the Silver Jubilee Fleet Review in June. The Royal Yacht *Britannia* provided the vantage point for the Queen and her family.

Above **The Queen and Prince Philip take a well-earned rest at Balmoral during Jubilee Year. Even Balmoral was not quite as peaceful as usual since photographers had for once been invited to invade the privacy. No 'at home' picture would be complete without a corgi.**

Opposite **Perhaps an even greater joy for the Queen than the affection shown her during the Jubilee celebrations in 1977 was the arrival of her first grandchild, Master Peter Phillips, on 15 November. After his christening at Buckingham Palace the two families gathered round to admire him.**

The young man who would one day inherit all these was meanwhile leaving the Navy, initially to launch the Queen's Silver Jubilee Appeal, which was dedicated to helping the young to help others and within a year had raised a record £16 million. On 15 November his sister gave the Queen what must have been one of her loveliest presents of Jubilee year, her first grandchild. Peter Phillips arrived at St Mary's Hospital, Paddington (the first royal baby born a commoner for five hundred years, just before his grandmother was about to hold an investiture. For once in her life she was just a few minutes late for an engagement, but her guests cheered when she apologised and told them why. Within a week there was another Jubilee baby when the Duchess of Gloucester gave birth to her first daughter, Lady Davina Windsor, who three years later was to have a sister, Lady Rose.

After the excitement of Jubilee Year, 1978 was fairly quiet. It saw the divorce by common consent of the Snowdons, which enabled the Queen's former brother-in-law to remarry shortly afterwards. Another marriage, even more fraught with complications, took place on 30 June, when the Queen's cousin, Prince Michael of Kent, married Baroness Marie-Christine von Reibnitz. Because she was a divorced Catholic and had expressed the intention of allowing any children she might have to be brought up as Anglicans, the couple were not allowed to marry in a Catholic church and opted instead for a civil ceremony in Vienna. Prince Michael felt obliged to renounce his place in the line of succession, but that was not to prevent his wife from playing a very active role as the newest recruit to the Royal Family.

The Queen and the Duke of Edinburgh had two Communist leaders to entertain at the Palace that year, President Tito of Yugoslavia, whom they had visited so enjoyably in 1972, and President Ceausescu of Romania, before they went to Canada with their youngest sons to see England bring in a good haul of gold medals at the Commonwealth Games in August.

Top, left **This little boy was carried away by his enthusiasm when he dashed up to present his bouquet to the Queen during her visit to Alderney in June 1978. Also on the itinerary was Jersey, where the Queen was able to compare the home-grown product with her own herd of Jerseys at Windsor.**

Above **In a fairly quiet year after the often frantic excitement of 1977 the Queen included a state visit to West Germany in her 1978 programme. Prince Philip seems fascinated by the other signatures in the visitors' book at Bonn Town Hall.**

Top, right **This colourful line-up was awaiting the Queen when she visited the Royal Tournament at Earl's Court on 19 July 1978. Along with other members of the Royal Family she is a regular visitor.**

Top, right Kenyan athlete Ben Jipcho was at Buckingham Palace on 26 July 1978 to receive from the Queen's hands the baton which was to be relayed to the eleventh Commonwealth Games in Edmonton, Canada. The Queen and the Duke were there with their two youngest sons in August to see England bring in a fine haul of gold medals.

Right In the lap of obvious luxury the Queen enjoys a moment of earnest conversation with her hosts in Kuwait during the royal tour of the Gulf States in February 1979. In some of them it was necessary to declare her an 'honorary man' in deference to the Islamic custom which keeps wives hidden from view.

The Royal Family undoubtedly wished that 1979 could have been as quiet a year as its predecessor, but that was not to be. They were caught up in both tragedy and intrigue. Tragedy came on a day which should have been one of pleasant enjoyment, Bank Holiday Monday, 27 August. The Queen was taking a well-earned rest at Balmoral after two particularly gruelling overseas tours, to the Gulf countries and to Africa, when news was phoned through that a Provisional IRA bomb had blasted to pieces a fishing boat in Mullaghmore harbour, killing its owner, Lord Mountbatten, and one of his twin grandsons. There were two more deaths in this awful incident and eighteen British soldiers were killed in another one at Warrenpoint on the same day. 'Uncle Dickie' had been such a friend of the family for so long, always at hand to confide in and be advised by, that there was a terrible bitterness and sense of loss experienced all round and not least by Prince Charles to whom he had been particularly close. Both the Queen and the Duke were at the state funeral in Westminster Abbey and the memorial service in St Paul's in December to hear their oldest son pay tribute to one of the great influences on his own life and one of the great men of our time.

Above **August Bank Holiday 1979 was a bitter day for the Royal Family for it witnessed the murder of Earl Mountbatten by the Provisional IRA. On 5 September he was accorded a state funeral at Westminster Abbey where Prince Charles read the lesson and all the Royal Family gathered to pay their last respects.**

Left **The Queen and Prince Philip walk in procession from Windsor Castle to St George's Chapel for the 1979 Order of the Garter service. King George VI made his daughter a Lady of the Order and her husband a Knight but on her accession the Queen became Sovereign of the Order.**

Right **In July 1979 the Queen was among those present at Westminster's Roman Catholic cathedral for a flower festival and is here seen admiring the Arundel Carpet of flowers in the company of Cardinal Basil Hume, Archbishop of Westminster.**

Opposite, inset **President Soeharto of Indonesia and Madame Soeharto were on a state visit to Britain when this photograph was taken in 1979. They were returning the Queen's hospitality with this banquet given in her honour at Claridge's Hotel in London.**

Opposite **The Queen's presence at the Lusaka Commonwealth Conference in August 1979 undoubtedly helped to iron out misunderstandings. She was greeted by her old friend President Kenneth Kaunda when she arrived at Lusaka airport with Prince Philip and Prince Andrew.**

Below **The Queen was about to meet some of her humbler subjects when she arrived at the Salvation Army's 'Hope Town' hostel in February 1980. After opening the home she talked to some of its residents about the problems of a lifestyle very different from her own.**

This year which saw a major figure leave the world's stage so tragically also saw the arrival on it of a major female one. When Mr Callaghan and his party lost the election on 3 May they paved the way for a piece of history to be made as Margaret Thatcher became Britain's first-ever woman Prime Minister. She soon had cause to value the wisdom, knowledge and experience of the other woman at the nation's head, not least because it was almost certainly the Queen's presence at the Lusaka Commonwealth Conference in July which did much to iron out misunderstandings between Britain and Kenneth Kaunda of Zambia, an old friend of the Queen's, and to pave the way for the successful outcome of the Lancaster House talks about the future of Rhodesia.

Towards the end of 1979 the press was presented with a story so sensational that it was almost beyond the imagination of Fleet Street to have dreamt it up. It was revealed that the man who from 1967 had been Keeper of the Queen's Pictures had confessed to British Security back in 1964 to being the so-called 'fourth man' in the Burgess–Maclean–Philby spy scandal. Whether the Queen had been privy to this information at the time will probably never be known, but acting under public pressure she felt obliged to strip the unfortunate Anthony Blunt of his knighthood.

Right Even at the age of nearly eighty the Queen Mother was a scene-stealer wherever she went and her daughter was happy to bask in the sunshine she spread around her. Here they are collecting their shamrock sprays before inspecting the Irish Guards at their annual St Patrick's Day Parade at Windsor.

Below Here the Queen meets another scene-stealer, Justin Henry, the young star of *Kramer vs Kramer*, which had its royal première on 17 March 1980. The two adult stars, Meryl Streep and Dustin Hoffman, seem graciously resigned to their supporting roles.

Below A family photograph taken in the land of her birth to celebrate the Queen Mother's eightieth birthday. The setting was the Palace of Holyroodhouse in Edinburgh where festivities got under way in July.

As one star fell to earth another continued to shine as brightly as ever. The Queen's mother had, indeed, been a star for nigh on eighty years, a fact which was recognised when the nation came to celebrate her birthday at St Paul's on 15 July. The Queen, with her unerring sense of what is fitting, commanded that the place of honour in the procession be accorded to her mother, and so, accompanied in the State Landau by Prince Charles, the Queen Mother arrived last at the Cathedral, on whose steps she turned to give one of those beguiling smiles to the crowds assembled below. It was a very happy occasion shared by the Royal Family with the nation, all honouring a lady described by her favourite grandson as 'one of those extraordinarily rare people whose touch can turn everything to gold'.

Left One of her favourite photographers, Norman Parkinson, took this highly original photograph of the Queen Mother with her two daughters to celebrate her eightieth birthday. The matching dark blue satin capelets were specially made for the occasion.

Opposite, top After the Queen Mother's eightieth birthday service at St Paul's the Royal Family gathered at Buckingham Palace for this commemorative photograph. One of the corgis was determined not to be left out of the celebrations.

Above The year 1980 was one for particular celebration by both the Royal Family and the nation for it was the year of the Queen Mother's eightieth birthday. On 15 July a service of thanksgiving took place at St Paul's Cathedral, with the Queen Mother occupying the place of honour.

Right The St Paul's Eightieth Birthday Thanksgiving Service was a little premature for the Queen Mother did not actually reach this milestone until 4 August. She was looking every bit as radiant as usual when she came to the gate of Clarence House to acknowledge the birthday wishes of the crowds and accept countless posies from small children.

Prince Charles showed his literary form in earnest that year when his book *The Old Man of Lochnagar* was published. It was a fairy story set in Scotland and written for his two younger brothers many years previously. It now looked as if the prospect of Prince Charles having children of his own to read it to was growing nearer as press speculation about his relationship with Lady Diana Spencer heightened.

The Prince was approaching his mid-thirties and his parents must have been worrying about whether he would ever find a girl he loved who would be acceptable to the nation and the Commonwealth and would be willing to shoulder the burden of being queen one day. Lady Diana, with her engaging personality, seemed an ideal choice. Though not herself royal she had in fact more lines of descent from King Charles II than the Prince himself. Her family had been friendly with royalty for generations, and the Princess's father Earl Spencer was a godson of Queen Mary and had been Equerry to the Queen's father and to the Queen herself. Though sadly his marriage to the daughter of Lord and Lady Fermoy had broken up in 1969, there was a happy connection on the maternal side in that Lady Fermoy had for long been one of the Queen Mother's ladies-in-waiting.

It was hardly a surprise to anyone when the following news came from Buckingham Palace on 24 February 1981: 'It is with the greatest pleasure that The Queen and The Duke of Edinburgh announce the betrothal of their beloved son, The Prince of Wales, to the Lady Diana Spencer, daughter of the Earl Spencer and the Honourable Mrs Shand Kydd.' Just over a month later the Prince was at a Privy Council meeting at Buckingham Palace during which his mother gave her official approval to his marriage.

Left The Queen was back at Westminster Abbey for the distribution of 1981's royal Maundy Money. One of the innovations of her reign has been the holding of the ceremony at various provincial cathedrals and abbeys, though the posies and the Yeomen of the Guard are unchanging features.

Opposite There were more family celebrations on 24 February 1981 when it was announced that the royal family's ranks were to be swelled by the addition of a young lady with all the charm and star quality of the Queen Mother. Obviously delighted, the Queen posed with her son and Lady Diana Spencer at Buckingham Palace on the day the Privy Council gave its formal consent to their marriage.

Before she could enjoy her son's wedding there were two rather nasty and unprecedented incidents for the Queen to endure, symptomatic of the violent direction in which the world was moving. She was hardly aware of the first because the IRA bomb planted at the Sullom Voe oil terminal which she arrived in Shetland to inaugurate exploded before she appeared on the scene. The incident at the Trooping the Colour ceremony was more frightening. A seventeen-year-old youth, later charged under the Treason Act, pointed a replica pistol at the Queen as she rode out of the Mall towards the parade ground and fired six blank shots from a distance of only about fifteen yards. The Queen had to struggle to control her frightened horse, a task made more difficult because she always rides side-saddle on these occasions, while the crowd quickly overpowered her assailant. The cool courage and presence of mind with which she reacted were by now what people had come to expect of this remarkable lady.

Above, left **King Khaled of Saudi Arabia, whose country the Queen had visited during her Gulf tour of 1979, was her guest in London in June 1981. At the glittering banquet which he arranged at Claridge's to honour his hostess all eyes were on Lady Diana Spencer, just embarking on her royal career.**

Above, right **A delightfully informal picture of Prince Philip and Pope John Paul II having an amiable exchange of views during the state visit to the Vatican in October 1980. The Queen wears the long black dress and veil required by Vatican protocol.**

Right **A terrifying moment in the Mall. As the Queen struggles to control her frightened horse Burmese she is not to know that the shots fired at her on the way to the 1981 Trooping the Colour ceremony are blanks. The angry crowd helped police to arrest her seventeen-year-old assailant.**

Above The Queen proudly presents her son with his award after a polo match at Windsor in July 1981 only three days before his wedding. His future bride must have been worrying about whether her husband would appear at the altar in one piece for he had already been thrown twice on the racecourse by his horse Good Prospect.

Right Two families just united by marriage watch proudly as the Prince of Wales leads his bride from the altar to the Great West Door of St Paul's Cathedral to acknowledge the cheers of the people before the ceremonial procession to Buckingham Palace.

The Queen herself recognised that there was another kind of courage as well as the physical. This year had been nominated the Year of the Disabled and in her Christmas message film was shown of her presenting cars to disabled people in the gardens of Buckingham Palace. Few would have denied that she too possessed the moral courage she so readily praised in others.

There were two infant female additions to the Royal Family before the more glamorous adult one in July. Princess Michael of Kent gave birth in April to a daughter, Gabriella, a sister for Lord Frederick Windsor, born two years earlier. Then, on 15 May 1981, Princess Anne presented the Queen with her first grand-daughter, only a month before her own thirty-first birthday was to be celebrated with a dinner party and dance given by her parents at Windsor. Zara Anne Elizabeth Phillips was baptised at the castle just two days before her uncle's wedding.

Prince Philip had attended a fairly boisterous stag party the night before his wedding, but for Charles things were to be more sedate as well as more spectacular. Along with half a million Londoners and a host of kings, queens, presidents and other dignitaries, he was in Hyde Park with his parents to watch the greatest firework display in Britain for over two hundred years.

Lady Diana had decided on an early night instead and appeared fresh and beautiful as she set out with her father in the coach from Clarence House where she had been staying as the Queen Mother's guest. The Queen and the Duke travelled to St Paul's in each other's company, but on the return journey the Queen was chatting animatedly to her old friend Earl Spencer while her husband accompanied the bride's mother. In the cathedral the eyes of the world had of course been on the two young people and there was a particularly moving moment when, on their way out, the couple stopped, the Prince to bow, his new wife to curtsey, before their monarch.

Below In the company of the bride's father, her old friend Earl Spencer, the Queen drives back to Buckingham Palace after the wedding service on 29 July. The Duke rode in another carriage with the bride's mother, the Hon Mrs Shand Kydd.

Right One of the formal group photographs taken by Lord Lichfield in the Throne Room at Buckingham Palace after the Royal Wedding. Among the many royal guests were the Kings of Sweden, Belgium and Norway and the Queens Regnant of the Netherlands and Denmark.

After the wedding breakfast and the obligatory photo session and balcony appearances the couple departed to the quiet retreat of Broadlands, just as the Prince's parents had done thirty-four years earlier; but in the less austere 1980s the second half of the honeymoon was in the sunshine of a Mediterranean cruise, not the November chill of a Scottish estate. It was to the Scottish estate that the newlyweds returned, however, to spend an autumn holiday with the Queen and Prince Philip before the parents left for another of their long tours, this time to Australia, New Zealand and Sri Lanka.

Above **The happy scene on the balcony as bride and groom acknowledge the good wishes of the thousands gathered in the Mall. They have been joined by their parents, the two maternal grandmothers, Princes Edward and Andrew, and the pages and bridesmaids.**

Left **After their honeymoon the royal newlyweds were able to join the Queen and the Duke of Edinburgh at Balmoral for their annual holiday. The customary visit to the Braemar Gathering gave Scottish subjects their chance to have a good look at their future queen, beautifully and diplomatically dressed in a black tam-o'-shanter and red check suit.**

Right **After the excitement of her eldest son's wedding the Queen had only a brief rest before she was off on another lengthy tour, this time taking her to Australia, New Zealand and Sri Lanka.**

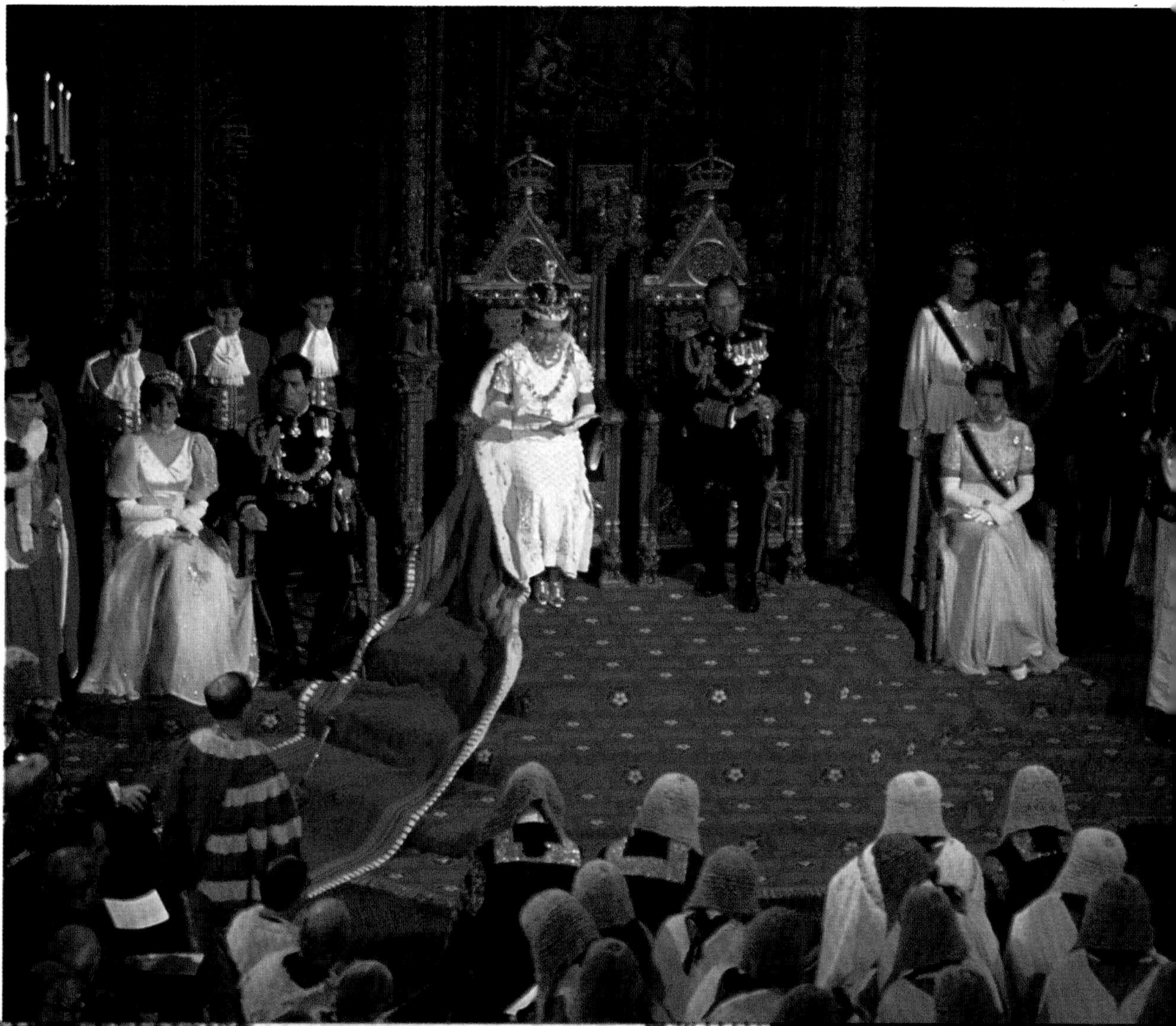

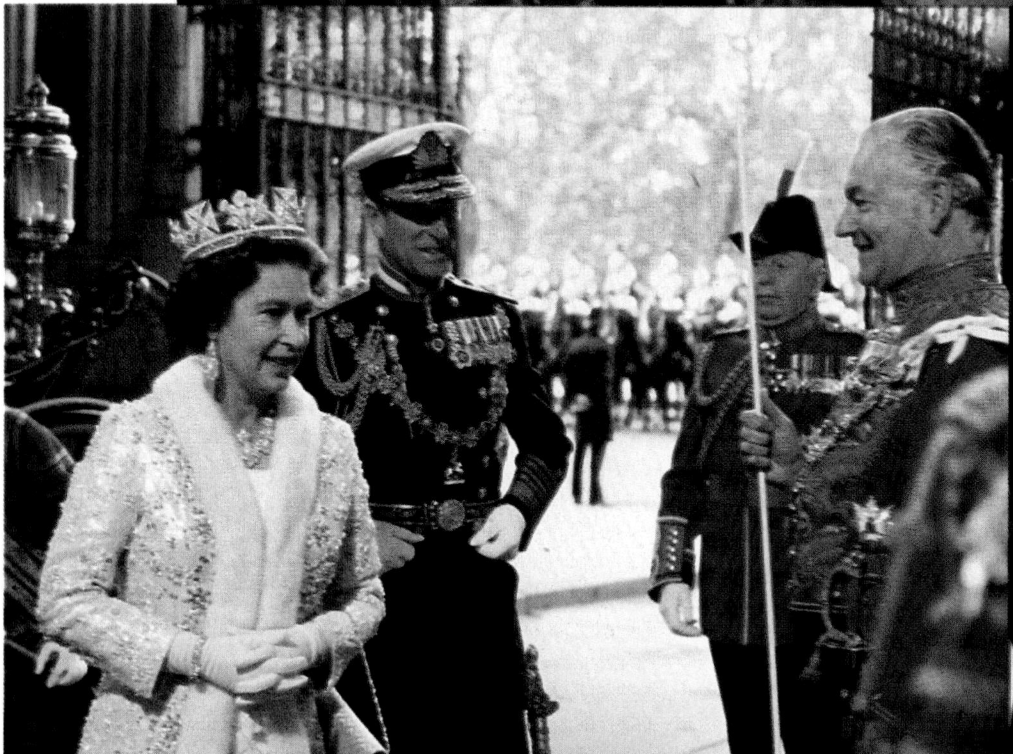

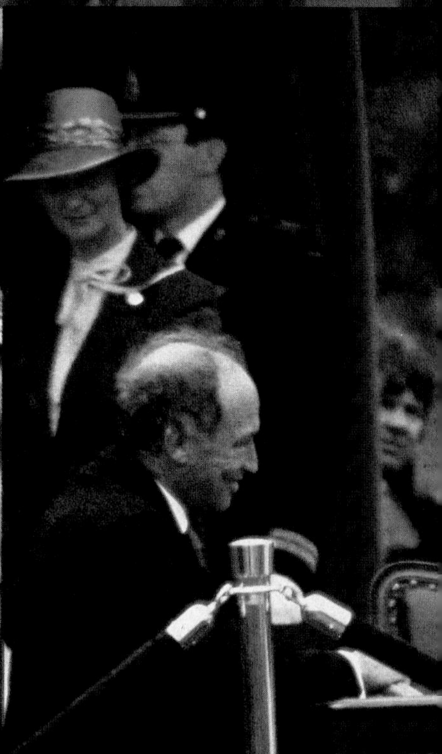

Opposite, top The State Opening of Parliament on 4 November 1981 was an even more glittering event than usual for the new Princess of Wales was making her first appearance at the ceremony. She sat with her husband on one side of the enthroned Queen and Prince Philip while Princess Anne and her husband took up their positions on the other.

Opposite, bottom left An unusual view of the Queen and her husband as they arrive for 1981's State Opening of Parliament. In the Robing Room the Queen exchanges her diamond and pearl tiara for the much heavier and priceless Imperial State Crown before walking in procession to the House of Lords.

Right A delighted Queen re-opened the Temperate House at Kew Gardens on 13 May 1982.

Left An historic day for Canada. Prime Minister Pierre Trudeau looks on as the Queen signs the Royal Proclamation enacting Canada's Constitution Act at an open-air ceremony on Ottawa's Parliament Hill. As Trudeau himself said, on this April day she 'severed this last colonial link with Britain'.

It was obvious even before the wedding that a new star was in the ascendant and the Press now had eyes only for Princess Diana. It was perhaps something of a relief for the Queen personally to have the limelight lifted from her a little. With the addition of his lovely wife, the Heir to the Throne had acquired a new glamour. Everyone the world over wanted a piece of the magic and while Charles took his wife round to meet the people, the Queen continued with her own lifelong work for the Commonwealth. An important change was taking place in the relations between Canada and Britain and the Queen was in Ottawa in April to sign, under the watchful eyes of Prime Minister Trudeau, the proclamation enacting Canada's Constitution Act, which finally terminated the power of the British Parliament to rubber-stamp legislation for Canada. It seemed a very belated coming of age for a rather sophisticated country.

Canada's neighbours have always been just about as royalist as republicans can be and had lapped up every detail of the Royal Wedding. Representing the President on that occasion had been his wife Nancy, but both Reagans were able to visit the Queen at Windsor in June 1982. The accent was on informality, to the extent of hostess and guest riding together in Windsor's Home Park without any hard hats, as the safety-conscious were quick to point out. The Queen and President Reagan knew more serious dangers, as did Pope John Paul II, who had been the victim of an assassination attempt the very day the Queen narrowly missed danger at Sullom Voe when a bomb exploded. The month before the Reagan visit the Pope had been a guest of the Queen and had seemed fully recovered, the old self whom she had met back in 1980 when she made the first state visit of a reigning British monarch to the Vatican. All the talk now was of reconciliation and the day after his reception at the Palace the Pope was preaching in Canterbury Cathedral alongside the Archbishop of Canterbury and in the presence of the Prince of Wales. Only a few years earlier such an event would have seemed unthinkable.

Truth must have appeared stranger than fiction to a lot of people in July when they picked up their daily papers and read that a Buckingham Palace intruder had actually found his way into the Queen's bedroom. She had woken just after seven to find herself confronted by a barefoot man in t-shirt and jeans who proceeded to sit on her bed brandishing a broken glass ashtray and pouring out his troubles. The Queen managed to phone for help, but sounded so calm that no one imagined for a moment that it was an emergency and it was eight minutes before the police on duty at the Palace arrived on the scene, by which time the Queen had persuaded the intruder to join a footman for cigarettes in one of the pantries. Her courage and presence of mind had again been extraordinary, though most of her 'bodyguards' emerged from the incident with very red faces. The intruder, who turned out to have meant no harm to the Queen whom he greatly admired, was eventually sent for psychiatric treatment.

Above The Queen is always pleased to meet her Chelsea Pensioners and especially so in 1982 when the Royal Hospital celebrated the three hundredth anniversary of its founding by Charles II. Like the old soldiers, the Queen wears on her lapel a sprig of oak leaves in memory of her ancestor's escape from capture by hiding in a tree after the battle of Worcester in 1651.

Left The 'special relationship' between the United States and Great Britain seemed very much intact when President Reagan and his wife Nancy visited Windsor Castle in June 1982. The ex-star of cowboy films was able to join his hostess for a ride in the Home Park while the Duke drove Mrs Reagan round in one of his carriages.

Right Pope John Paul II, history's most travelled pope, was in Britain in May 1982 and the Queen's guest at Buckingham Palace on the 28th. They talked alone together for forty-five minutes and film of the meeting was shown on television.

officers

If events at home seemed to be more unbelievable by the minute, foreign affairs were hardly less extraordinary. Not many years previously it would also have seemed unthinkable that Britain would become involved in a war with a South American country over some islands near the South Pole which most British people had never heard of, but such was the now familiar course of history. Like many another mother, the Queen worried about the safety of her son, for Prince Andrew was now in the Royal Navy and serving on HMS *Invincible* in the Falklands. As he was later to describe quite graphically himself, the Prince had some very narrow escapes, and his parents and sister must have greeted him with some relief when on 17 September his ship sailed into Spithead, the war over, for a joyous reunion. Prince Edward could not be there because he had just taken up a post as junior house tutor at Wanganui Collegiate in New Zealand, another member of the family doing his best to cement Commonwealth relations.

Another great happiness in an otherwise rather troubled year was the birth on 21 June 1982, at St Mary's Hospital, Paddington, of the Prince and Princess of Wales's first son, baptised William Arthur Philip Louis, at Buckingham Palace on his great-grandmother's eighty-second birthday. He was a noisy baby whose cries seemed to be stilled only when his mother's little finger was given him to suck. Film of the occasion did much to strengthen affection for what almost seemed a family as ordinary as any.

Above For the Queen, like thousands of other mothers with sons serving in the Falklands, it was a moment of profound relief when the bulk of the British forces could return home. Prince Andrew's ship HMS *Invincible* docked at Portsmouth on 17 September 1982 to allow one of the happiest of Royal Family reunions.

Opposite, top left It is not often that the Queen gets a welcome like this but she seems to be enjoying the novelty vastly. She and the Duke were each paddled ashore in a dugout canoe when visiting one of their Pacific islands in October 1982 and then carried in procession on the shoulders of the burly islanders.

Opposite, bottom One of the happiest events of 1982 – the christening of the second in line of succession, William Arthur Philip Louis, at Buckingham Palace. Mother knows the best way to still a noisy baby's cries while grandfather and great-grandmother look on with fascination.

Right At the 1982 Commonwealth Games held in Brisbane medallists were privileged to receive their awards from the Queen. Here, at one of the ladies' swimming events, she is stretching up to place the ribbon round the neck of England's June Croft. The winner, Tracy Wickham of Australia, has already received her medal.

214

Even the warm affection of the American people could not disguise the atrociousness of the weather when the Queen arrived in the United States the following spring. There were also pro-IRA demonstrations to contend with and the tragedy of a road accident which killed three of the Secret Service men assigned to her. She nevertheless managed to find her way through torrential rain for a visit to the President's ranch and returned the hospitality with a dinner on *Britannia* to celebrate the Reagans' thirty-first wedding anniversary on 4 March 1983.

There were reunions with other international figures, among them President Mitterand and the King and Queen of Tonga, all visitors to the Palace, and Mrs Gandhi, met again during a tour which also took the Queen back to Treetops, the lodge in Kenya where she became queen. Mrs Gandhi, like her guest, had 'inherited' her country from a wise and respected father and her assassination the following year robbed the Commonwealth of an accumulation of experience and knowledge probably equalled only by that of the Queen herself. Recognising another kind of human excellence, the Queen was able while in India to award the Order of Merit to Mother Teresa, the Catholic nun who has devoted a lifetime to the care of the dying and destitute in the slums of Calcutta. No doubt reports from Prince Charles about his visit had kindled the Queen's interest even more than the great publicity which had followed the award of the Nobel Peace Prize to Mother Teresa.

Above **During the royal visit to the United States in 1983 the weather was atrocious when the Queen and the Duke visited the Reagans' ranch.**

Right **This visit to Kenya in November 1983 must have stirred both sad and happy memories. With hunter Dick Prickett, the Queen and the Duke walk past Treetops, the game lodge where she spent her last carefree hours as a Princess before learning of the death of her father.**

Left It looks like the Far East but these oriental musicians were in fact performing for the Queen in Vancouver during her visit to Canada in March 1983. The Queen's jaunty straw boater was an interesting variation on her usual style of hat.

Below Already recognised by many as perhaps the world's greatest living saint, Mother Teresa of Calcutta receives the Order of Merit from the hands of the Queen, a further tribute to her work among the dying and destitute of India's slums.

Above Two of the longest-surviving influences within the Common-wealth meet in India during the 1983 Commonwealth Tour. Within a year of this encounter an assassin's bullet would have claimed Mrs Gandhi's life, hours before she was to have entertained the Queen's daughter in Delhi.

Left The Christmas Day gathering on the steps of St George's Chapel after the 1982 service. For the Queen the year had witnessed two things to be particularly thankful for, the safe return of Prince Andrew from the Falklands and the arrival of the Prince and Princess of Wales's first son.

Below The Queen and Prince Philip bravely risked the dangers of the trouble-torn Middle East when they were the guests of King Hussein of Jordan and his American-born wife Queen Noor in March 1984. They were able to visit Petra, the ancient 'rose-red city' carved out of rock.

Opposite, top This exotic display was one of the many colourful sights to greet the royal visitors' eyes during their tour of India in 1983. The dancers were performing their skilful balancing act at the village of Devara Yamzal.

Opposite, bottom In the May of 1983 the Queen and the Duke of Edinburgh arrived at Stockholm aboard this splendid craft. King Carl Gustaf and Queen Silvia were there to welcome them to a country where royalty is treated so informally that Swedish women no longer curtsey to their own or visiting monarchs.

Left Another little face to be woven into the web of European royal connections. This is Princess Theodora, photographed in the arms of her mother Queen Anne-Marie of Greece after her Greek Orthodox christening in London in October 1983. Her father, exiled King Constantine, is closely related to Prince Philip and her mother is the sister of the Danish Queen.

Mrs Gandhi's assassination on 31 October 1984 and the attempt on Mrs Thatcher's life in the Brighton bombing earlier the same month were reminders, if any were needed, of the risk continually attendant upon all figures prominent in public life. The Queen's security was tightened after the Brighton outrage but she had already risked terrorist action when she visited Jordan in March. Prior to her arrival there was a bomb explosion in the capital Amman and the situation was so bad it was felt necessary to fit an anti-missile system to the plane transporting her around. It was a very short visit, but it stirred up some controversy as the Queen was inevitably drawn into Middle East politics. Most of her subjects would probably have shared the feelings of sympathy with the plight of the Palestinian people which the Queen expressed in a speech at a state banquet given in her honour, but there was some controversy over her reported comment of 'Depressing' when the Jordanians insisted on pointing out to her the Israeli settlement on the West Bank.

It was not to be an easy year abroad. More criticism awaited her in the autumn, this time in Canada where wide publicity was given to a few distasteful remarks about her appearance and manner, particularly unfair when made of one who cannot answer back. After more than three decades as the centre of attention, it was perhaps no surprise if the Queen occasionally looked a little tired and less than fascinated by the activities going on around her, and she had never pretended to be a fashion plate. As always, the vast majority rushed to her defence, grateful for the Queen's years of uncomplaining devotion to duty and for the fact that she represents values more than skin deep.

Fortunately there was very little controversy about the celebration of the fortieth anniversary of the D-Day landings in Normandy, for which the Queen and the Duke set sail on *Britannia* in June. Along with other European heads of state and President Reagan, she was to pay homage to those who died on Utah Beach before going on a happy walkabout among British veterans, overjoyed both to meet the Queen and comrades.

Above **Andrew Lloyd Webber received another fillip to his amazing career when the Queen attended a gala performance of his latest musical *Starlight Express* in March 1984.**

Below **Jayne Torvill and Christopher Dean had aleady raised the art of ice dancing to new heights with perfect scores at the Winter Olympics at Sarajevo when the Queen met them at their home town Nottingham during a visit in April 1984.**

Above **Prince Charles delighted
onlookers and press photographers
by his old-fashioned gallantry after a
match at the Guards Polo Club in
Windsor on 19 May 1984. The
Queen has found herself making
awards to members of her talented
family with amazing frequency.**

Below **The fortieth anniversary of
D-Day brought a distinguished
collection of Western leaders to Utah
Beach in Normandy in June 1984 as
well as many of the old soldiers who
took part in the landings. The
Queen and President Reagan were
there to represent the English-
speaking Allies.**

There was no doubt about the Queen's continuing popularity in Britain itself where the Greater London Council, bowing to public pressure, invited the Queen to open the Thames Barrier, another of Britain's spectacular engineering achievements. 'Red' Ken Livingstone, leader of the Greater London Council, was a genial host, and his mother, perhaps more ardently royalist than her son, was delighted to be presented to her monarch on the occasion. People in the north of England had had their opportunity a week earlier when the Queen, again accompanied by the Duke, was in Liverpool to open the International Garden Festival, designed to bring some hope to an area blighted by unemployment.

The Queen's new daughter-in-law was also brightening up the scene, becoming the darling of the fashion writers as well as a world-class superstar. Still at the beginning of her royal career, but with all the energy and enthusiasm of youth, she yet has much to learn from the sterling example of her mother-in-law. In one respect at least a similarity is already apparent, for with Prince Charles she is presenting that same youthful pattern of happy family life which Elizabeth and Philip had presented to the nation back in the late 1940s and 1950s.

Above **Prince Philip demonstrates his skill at four-in-hand driving for the benefit of his wife and two grandchildren, Peter and Zara Phillips, at one of the horse shows at Windsor in 1984. He took up driving after an injury forced him to give up playing polo.**

Left **London acquired an unusual landmark in May 1984 when the Queen opened the Thames flood barrier, seen in the background of this picture. It was another remarkable feat of British engineering skill which, besides its practical value, was to bring the tourists flocking to east London.**

Opposite, top **Prince Edward, the most scholarly of the Queen's children, was the second one to go to university, choosing Cambridge, but Jesus College rather than Prince Charles's Trinity. In 1984 his parents went down to see for themselves how he was getting on with his history studies.**

Opposite, bottom **Every November the Queen comes to the Cenotaph in London's Whitehall to lay a wreath in memory of the nation's war dead, while other royal ladies watch the ceremony from a Home Office balcony. In 1984, with the Falklands War still so fresh in the memory, Remembrance Day had particular poignancy.**

Below The Queen seemed relaxed and extremely happy after the Christening of fourteen-year-old Prince Harry at Windsor Castle. Perhaps she was still smiling at the antics of older brother Prince William who had been chasing his cousin Zara Phillips round the Archbishop of Canterbury's legs.

Left Lord Snowdon recorded Prince William's floorshow for posterity as he entertained family and godparents.

The family of three happily became a family of four when on 15 September the Princess of Wales gave birth to her second son, just in time for the Queen to see him before she set off on her Canadian tour. After Prince Henry Charles Albert David had been christened at St George's Chapel, Windsor, in December there were the usual official photographs, taken as so often in the past by Lord Snowdon. As the older brother cheekily stole the scene the Queen's mind must have gone back irresistibly to the christening of Princess Anne when Prince Charles had behaved in a very similar way. Boys will be boys, and one wheel had certainly come full circle in the Queen's life in a delightfully satisfying way.

Left The Queen's working day almost invariably starts with a couple of hours' attention to the contents of her morocco dispatch boxes, seen on the right of this picture. They contain important official documents which have to be read and signed and are delivered to her daily wherever she is, even, as in this instance, at her Sandringham home.

Most of the Queen's days follow in part a fairly fixed pattern, not dissimilar to that followed by her dutiful and hardworking grandfather George V. At 7.45 her maid enters the Queen's bedroom at the Palace and draws back the curtains before presenting Her Majesty with her early-morning tea, the daily papers and any letters from personal friends that have arrived via the Palace's Post Office. During breakfast, after the Duke has added his own comments on world affairs to those broadcast on the BBC's news programme, the Queen will be honoured at 9 o'clock with a fifteen-minute serenade from a lone bagpiper outside the dining-room window, a well-loved tradition dating back to Queen Victoria's time.

At about ten the Queen will retire to her high-ceilinged office cum sitting-room overlooking the lawns and trees of the Palace gardens. Surrounded by dogs, vases of flowers and family photographs, she will settle down to an hour or two's paper work. The first member of the Royal Household to see her will be her Private Secretary. He is responsible for planning her schedules and drafting speeches, and also helps the Queen 'do her boxes'. These are the battered dispatch boxes of red morocco which follow her around the country, arriving virtually every morning and evening.

They contain the key Foreign Office cables, those with reports from British ambassadors and Ministers in foreign countries and any replies from the Foreign Office. All the documents must be read and initialled or signed. There are also copies of memoranda for consideration by the Cabinet and reports of their meetings, together with the latest issue of Hansard so that she is up to date with what is going on in Parliament. To keep her informed of world affairs there are letters from her ambassadors and governors-general and reports on the various Commonwealth countries, together with the minutes of important conferences. Fortunately the Queen is a speedy worker, with a marvellous knack of picking out at a glance the most important point in a document. Even so, she may have to spend two or three hours of the day reading these state papers and so keeping herself abreast of world and home affairs. This is work that can be done by her and her alone.

As well as her boxes, the Queen has a mass of personal correspondence to deal with. She receives on average two hundred letters a day and considerably more on special occasions – at the height of Jubilee fervour in London, for example, she received three thousand five hundred letters on one day alone. Of course she has staff to help her deal with these and send out the increasing number of royal telemessages to those subjects celebrating their one hundredth birthdays who are not forgotten even with this enormous work load.

Below **Even the sea is no obstacle to the arrival of the red boxes. In 1972 Lord Lichfield was lucky enough to get this unusual shot of the Queen at work on the Royal Yacht** *Britannia* **with Sir Martin Charteris, who was her Private Secretary from 1950 until he retired in 1977 to become Provost of Eton.**

If the Queen is at home all day the chances are that the latter half of the morning will be devoted to an investiture, a Privy Council Meeting or a series of Audiences. Investitures are usually held in Buckingham Palace's splendid Ball Room, to the accompaniment of military bandsmen playing popular melodies. Privy Council meetings occur slightly more frequently – about twenty times a year – though only a small number of the over 300 Privy Councillors, who include Prince Philip and all the Cabinet, are likely to be present. Audiences take place in the first-floor Audience Room and the Queen usually receives eight or nine people in a morning for about ten minutes each. They might include a British or foreign ambassador, a judge, a civil servant or perhaps a bishop.

One or other of the people received in audience may be invited to stay for lunch, perhaps for one of the informal lunches started in 1956. If so, they will join fewer than a dozen other guests for pre-lunch drinks in the Bow Room, where the scurry of corgis will herald the arrival of the Queen and her husband. She may have a sherry or soft drink with her guests before the whole party adjourns for a four-course lunch at the oval table in the 1844 Room. If she is not entertaining the Queen will have a very simple, almost meagre,

Above **Buckingham Palace by no means provides the Queen with a place of retreat from public duties. She has to entertain important visitors there, though this can be an undisguised pleasure when they are old friends like Queen Beatrix and Prince Claus and bring with them the most acceptable of gifts. In a rare view of official present-giving, the horse was being paraded in the courtyard of the Palace during the Dutch couple's state visit in November 1982.**

Above **Cameras rarely penetrate behind the stout walls of Buckingham palace, but in 1969 BBC and ITA film crews were there shooting *Royal Family* when the new American ambassador Walter Annenberg (centre) arrived to present his credentials to the Queen. Among others regularly received in audience are judges, bishops, civil servants, and British ambassadors reporting back to the Queen at the end of their overseas postings.**

lunch in the company of Prince Philip, unless he has an engagement elsewhere, in which case she may well lunch alone.

Buckingham Palace is usually a hive of activity on Tuesday afternoons because this is the time set aside for the Queen's dress designers and milliners. Their sessions with her start at 2.30 and may go on for more than two hours. The Queen will first approve designs and select fabrics. There will then be three or four fittings for each garment, carried out in the Queen's dressing-room, which is fitted with triple mirrors and dressing tables. Helping and advising the Queen and the fitters will be the formidable Margaret MacDonald, known as Bobo, who has been with the Queen for over half a century, first as nursemaid, then as dresser, and who is perhaps the only person outside the family she can really talk to.

As for so many of her subjects, afternoon tea in her sitting-room is for the Queen a time-honoured ritual, as well as a private family occasion. Her Page of the Presence wheels in a trolley laden with thin bread and butter, and perhaps egg-and-cress sandwiches, muffins and gingerbread. The Queen is very particular about her tea, which she drinks lukewarm and makes herself, using a favourite Darjeeling blend and scorning tea bags. She pays the same careful attention to the afternoon feeding of her dogs, whose meat, gravy and biscuits she mixes herself before distribution to the hungry animals waiting by the white plastic sheet in the corridor.

As well as the afternoon fittings, another regular feature of Tuesdays is the hour-long meeting with the Prime Minister in the early evening to discuss topics prepared by their two Private Secretaries. The Queen may very well raise other subjects too for she is remarkably well-informed about politics and interested in all the latest Parliamentary gossip. However, her meetings with Mrs Thatcher, though in the relaxed setting of the sitting-room, have tended to be rather more formal and correct than some of those with earlier Prime Ministers.

Most evenings the Queen likes nothing better than to kick her shoes off and relax, leaving the Duke of Edinburgh to attend the official functions and make the after-dinner speeches. There are occasions when she has to be out, perhaps at some gala performance or a première, and of course she is the centre of attraction as well as the hostess at any banquet given at Buckingham Palace and must dress the part. State banquets in honour of visiting monarchs and presidents are held in the Ball Room and run like clockwork. The Queen selects the menus and checks the arrangements, usually offering her visitors traditional English food, some of it from the Sandringham estate. As many as 150 extra staff may be hired specially from an employment agency to join the ranks of pages and footmen in their state livery. Victorian damask and masses of silver gilt decorate the tables, along with banks of flowers, making a truly splendid spectacle.

When there are just a few friends for dinner, the Queen will entertain them in the private dining-room next to her sitting-room, everyone seating themselves round the oval-shaped mahogany table laid with Georgian cutlery. If the Queen and the Duke have an evening alone together they will happily dispense with the staff and help themselves from silver dishes kept warm on hotplates.

There is a small kitchen attached to the royal apartments and the Queen may perhaps scramble herself some eggs and settle down to watch television with a meal on a tray. She likes documentaries and some outside broadcasts, especially anything to do with horses, wildlife, history or art. She also has a fondness for light music and comedy programmes such as *The Two Ronnies, Yes, Minister, Dad's Army* and *The Morecambe and Wise Show*. If she makes a private visit to the theatre it will probably be a light comedy or musical revue that she chooses, and she hardly need venture out to a cinema as Buckingham Palace has one of its own showing all the latest films, for staff as well as family.

If the Queen wants a good read she will settle down contentedly with a Dick Francis thriller, a Hammond Innes adventure story or perhaps some contemporary autobiography, but she will be just as happy with the latest copy of *The Field* or *Sporting Life*. If she wants something more challenging there is always the most difficult of the *Daily Telegraph* crosswords or a jigsaw, but of course part of the evening may need to be occupied with work, catching up on the events in Parliament by means of the handwritten notes made daily for her by the Vice-Chamberlain of the Household, or dealing with those ever-present boxes.

Opposite, top **Another event the Queen does not travel far to attend is the start of the Commonwelth Games. Brendan Foster was at Buckingham Palace on 22 June 1983 to receive from the Queen's hands the baton to be relayed to Brisbane. If she cannot attend such Games meetings herself they are among the kind of events the Queen enjoys watching on television.**

Right The Queen likes nothing better than a quiet evening at home with her shoes off but this is not always possible. When a foreign or Commonwealth head of state is visiting, Buckingham Palace is often a hive of activity as staff prepare for a state banquet. On this occasion, in March 1981, the guest of honour was President Alhaji Shehu Shagari of Nigeria.

THE QUEEN AT SIXTY

Students at Evora gave the Queen a Walter Raleigh-style welcome when she visited their university during her 1985 state visit to Portugal. They laid down their cloaks for her to walk over, then placed a black academic robe round her shoulders, an honour that delighted her.

As the Queen celebrates her sixtieth birthday on 21 April 1986, people and nations around the world will give thanks for her selfless dedication to a lifetime of service, but perhaps few will realise just how great is the burden taken up so willingly. In a space so short it has only been possible to mention a selection of her overseas tours – tours which have exhausted officials accompanying her, not to mention the journalists reporting on them. 'How does she do it?' must be the question continually asked. She has covered vast distances using almost every kind of transport invented, shaking innumerable hands and managing to make everyone she meets feel special. On average, perhaps a tenth of the year may be spent abroad, either strengthening relationships with foreign powers during state visits or exercising her functions as Commonwealth Head and Queen of monarchies as diverse as Canada and Papua New Guinea.

Of course the Queen also meets foreign and Commonwealth representatives at home. She entertains visiting royalty and heads of state, usually at Buckingham Palace or Windsor Castle, as well as receiving foreign ambassadors and her own representatives in the Commonwealth before they leave to take up their posts abroad.

Below **In 1979 the nation was making supreme efforts in support of the Year of the Child and the Queen insisted on meeting as many of her smaller subjects as she could. The world's largest-ever party for deprived children, held in Hyde Park, gave the perfect opportunity.**

Right **The Royal Yacht** *Britannia* **was at anchor off the Californian coast during the Queen's tour of America in March 1983, which made it possible for her and Prince Philip to entertain President and Mrs Reagan on the occasion of their wedding anniversary.**

As Queen of the United Kingdom she has to make frequent public appearances throughout the length of the land, visiting hospitals and schools, touring industrial areas, opening new buildings, attending film and stage performances, presenting prizes at sporting events such as the Cup Final – the list of functions at which she may appear is endless. She is particularly assiduous in attending events organised by the many bodies to whom she lends distinction by her patronage. The Queen is also 'at home' for the thousands of British and Commonwealth citizens invited to meet her and her family at the garden parties given each year in the grounds of Buckingham Palace and the Palace of Holyroodhouse.

Opposite Royal garden parties give the Queen a chance to meet a great many of her subjects in the pleasantest of surroundings. The grounds of Buckingham Palace usually provide the setting for several of these each year and the Queen is seen enjoying an animated conversation at one of those held here in July 1984.

Left The Queen's support of the arts spreads over a wide spectrum. The Royal Variety Show is a highlight of any year and nowadays is usually televised to an audience of millions. It gives singers such as Julia McKenzie, seen here at the 1983 event, and other variety artistes some of the crowning moments in brilliant careers.

Below A visit from the Queen brings delight to old as well as young, and professional cameramen have plenty of competition from the amateurs. These lucky onlookers caught the Queen in a very happy summery mood after a visit to Westminster Cathedral's Flower Festival in 1979.

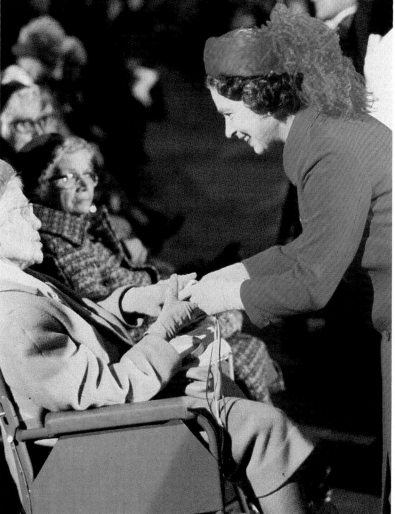

Above The presence of the Queen gives the ultimate dignity to any important occasion. She expressed not only the gratitude of a nation for the life of a great man but also the feelings of her family as she unveiled a statue to Lord Mountbatten on 2 November 1983 in the presence of the Prime Minister and the Royal Family.

Left Every year, on the Thursday before Easter, the Queen distributes specially minted Maundy Money to elderly men and women equal in number to her age. The ceremony is one of the most ancient in the Christian Church and commemorates Christ's washing of his disciples' feet.

Opposite The first public engagement of the Queen after her accession was at Westminster Abbey where she distributed the first Maundy Money of the new reign. One of her innovations has been the holding of the ceremony at cathedral churches outside the capital. In 1985 it was the turn of Ripon Cathedral to be so honoured and she is seen here with the Dean.

The garden parties are, of course, not the only events which take place annually and at which the Queen has to play the leading role. There is the distribution of the Royal Maundy Money when specially minted coins are distributed to elderly people equal in number to the Queen's age. The ceremony, dating back to the eleventh century, was traditionally held at Westminster Abbey, but during the present reign it has sensibly been held at various other cathedrals and abbeys so that people outside the capital can share the occasion.

As Sovereign of all the British Orders of Knighthood the Queen annually attends a number of their religious services, most notably those connected with the six hundred-year-old Order of the Garter, held at St George's Chapel, Windsor, and the Order of the Thistle, most ancient of the Scottish orders of chivalry, the services of which are held in St Giles' Cathedral, Edinburgh. Prince Charles was invested and installed as a Knight of the Garter by the Queen in 1968 and frequently accompanies his grandmother, a Lady of the Garter, in the annual procession from Windsor Castle to the Chapel. He is Great Master of another ancient order, the Order of the Bath, and was installed as such by his mother on the Order's two hundred and fiftieth anniversary in 1975.

Opposite Press cameras are not present at Palace investitures, which take place about fourteen times a year. This photograph, taken in New Zealand during the 1974 tour of Australasia, gives a seldom-seen view of the Queen bestowing a knighthood.

Below On her accession the Queen became Sovereign of all the British Orders of Knighthood, one of which is the Order of St Michael and St George, whose service she is seen arriving for in July 1984.

Overleaf **As well as being one of the great public events of the year, the Trooping the Colour ceremony is also something of a family occasion. Prince Charles and Prince Philip usually ride in the procession and nowadays there are young grandchildren to share the excitement of the balcony appearances.**

The Queen does of course create new knights, whose names are among those on the Honours Lists issued from Buckingham Palace on New Year's Eve and on her official birthday. The distinguished men and women chosen for honours attend one of the fourteen investitures held annually, where their decorations and medals are presented to them by the Queen, while knights must kneel before the monarch to have the royal sword lain on either shoulder according to ancient tradition.

On her official birthday, a Saturday in June, there is the popular Trooping the Colour ceremony when the Queen rides out from Buckingham Palace along the Mall to Horseguards Parade to review the Household Division in their splendid ceremonial uniforms. As Sovereign she is commander-in-chief of all the Armed Forces of the Crown, so is frequently called upon to review the representatives of all three Services. Whether standing on the deck of *Britannia* sailing among the ships of the Home Fleet or being driven along in the back of an Army landrover or walking the length of a line of planes, she is as much the unifying symbol as when, a small black-coated figure, she comes to the Cenotaph in Whitehall in November to pay homage, on behalf of the nation, to those who gave their lives in two World Wars.

Above As commander-in-chief of all the Armed Forces of the Crown the Queen is frequently called upon to review representatives of the Army, the Navy and the Air Force. In May 1981 it was the turn of the 1st Battalion the Welsh Guards who were presented with new colours by their colonel-in-chief at Windsor.

Opposite The Trooping the Colour ceremony is held annually on a Saturday in June and celebrates the Queen's 'official birthday'. She is seen here taking the salute at the gates of the Palace on her return from the 1984 event.

There are events which appear on the Queen's calendar year after year which are a great deal less solemn and which reflect her private interests. She is a regular visitor to the Chelsea Flower Show, as are other members of the Royal Family, and the Badminton Horse Trials in April, the Royal Windsor Horse Show and the Derby at Epsom in June. Horses are of course an abiding interest and it is entirely appropriate that it should be *Royal* Ascot Week in June. The Queen and members of her family customarily attend on all four days, the procession departing from Windsor Castle and going through Windsor Great Park to Ascot for the traditional drive along the course in open carriages before racing commences.

Below **The Queen has always loved flowers and likes to work surrounded by them. The annual visit to the Chelsea Flower Show is therefore no hardship and perhaps she got some new ideas about what might be planted in some of the royal gardens from her visit in May 1984.**

Above **Each day's racing during Royal Ascot Week in June is preceded by the royal procession up the course to the Royal Enclosure. At the 1983 meeting the Queen and the Duke of Edinburgh were as usual in the first of the open landaus, the Queen looking at her most sparkling in a delightful pink outfit to match the day's sunshine.**

Perhaps the most important annual event for a constitutional monarch is the State Opening of Parliament in November when the Queen, magnificent in her long robes and gown, drives in her State Coach through the capital to Westminster. Seated on her throne in the Lords she declares Parliament in session and reads the Queen's speech, written on the advice of the Ministers who govern in her name. She is committed to impartiality where politics are concerned though she has to be informed and consulted about all aspects of national life and no doubt lends the wisdom of her experience at the weekly audiences with her Prime Minister and at frequent meetings with other senior public servants. As Head of State she does still have the right to summon, prorogue and dissolve Parliament and theoretically to choose the Prime Minister, but this latter function is exercised in accordance with advice given her and with due regard to the feeling of the House of Commons.

By the Queen's side at the Opening of Parliament is usually the Duke of Edinburgh, as always playing the secondary role. It has never been an easy one, but he has always tried to support his wife while maintaining his own interests and independence of mind. As consort he can in fact feel free to say far more controversial things than the Queen would contemplate, though she is by nature more discreet. He takes on his fair share of public engagements and overseas tours of his own, as well as being by the Queen's side on most of hers and during state visits and Commonwealth tours abroad. He has also given his name to an Award Scheme designed to encourage enterprise in young people and is passionate in his support of the World Wildlife Fund.

The Prince of Wales is steadily being groomed for the role that

Left One of the Queen's most important engagements of the year is the State Opening of Parliament in November. Although she is usually the centre of attraction media attention was concentrated on the Princess of Wales's new upswept hairstyle at the 1984 ceremony.

will one day be his. He too is usually present at the State Opening of Parliament and, like his father, rides in the Trooping the Colour ceremony. He has, on occasion, taken the Queen's place at the Remembrance Day Service and represented her at Commonwealth independence celebrations. He is a Privy Counsellor and now acts with others for the Queen while she is out of the country. Suggestions of abdication continue to be fiercely rejected by Buckingham Palace and the Queen still refuses to take things more easily even though she is at an age when most of her female subjects retire, but at least now a younger generation is able to relieve her of some of her heavy burden.

If the Queen Mother wanted to retire from public life there is very little possibility that she would be allowed to, so great is the affection in which she is held. Well into her eighties, she continues to perform public functions with that charm and dignity which have endeared her to millions. Prince Charles has written of his grandmother as 'the most wonderful example of fun, laughter, warmth, infinite security and, above all else, exquisite taste in so many things' and how she can bring 'happiness and comfort to people by her presence', and there can be no doubt that the Queen has also benefited from these qualities of her mother, many of

which she has inherited. Both mother and sister have been of particular comfort to Princess Margaret in her sometimes troubled life. Between the two sisters there is a very close bond of affection in spite of the differences in their natures. The Princess plays her part by attending many official functions and helping her sister to entertain important overseas visitors, particularly valuable support when the Duke of Edinburgh is away on one of his tours. She also represents the Queen abroad, most keenly perhaps at any ceremonies held in her beloved West Indies.

Like Princess Margaret, Princess Anne has been brought up in the shadow of an older sibling, but has nevertheless managed to follow a very distinctive path of her own. Her equestrian successes have delighted the Queen and now she is devoting herself with equal energy and enthusiasm to her work for charities, most notably The Save the Children Fund, and winning universal admiration for her courage and plain speaking. In terms of royal engagements she is also one of the most hard-working of the Royal Family. Her younger brothers are still pursuing their careers and will not perhaps be so heavily drawn into the round of royal duties, though as long as they remain eligible bachelors they will undoubtedly go on providing fodder for the gossip columnists.

There is never a day of complete rest for the Queen for her boxes, and sometimes indeed her ministers, reach her even at her holiday homes. While the larger part of the year is spent at Buckingham Palace, with weekends at Windsor, only twenty-five miles away, the Queen always spends some time away from the capital, at her official Scottish residence 'the Palace of Holyroodhouse in Edinburgh' or at one of her two private homes, Sandringham in Norfolk and Balmoral on Scotland's Deeside.

January finds the Royal Family at Sandringham, originally acquired by Queen Victoria and Prince Albert for their eldest son, later Edward VII. He spent much of his time there and the house had been altered considerably by the time his son George V was making his first Christmas broadcast from it. George VI loved the place and particularly enjoyed the excellent shooting it provided. It was appropriate that he should have spent his last hours there and that his body lay in state in the little Sandringham church before being transported to London for the funeral.

At Sandringham and Balmoral the Queen probably comes closest to being what she would most like to have been, just an ordinary countrywoman surrounded by dogs and horses. As the public can now discover for themselves, Sandringham House is set in a large estate and the Queen is a farmer here as well as at Windsor and Balmoral which between them have five thousand acres of agricultural land. Farm produce from Sandringham, greater in quantity now than ever before, either goes up to London to be consumed at Buckingham Palace or is sold commercially. Amongst the other 'produce' of Sandringham are horses, dogs and pigeons, for it is here that the royal stud, the royal kennels and the royal pigeon lofts are situated. At Sandringham and nearby Wolferton the Queen's racehorses, carriage horses, polo ponies and event horses are bred, most distinguished in the past perhaps being Doublet on which Princess Anne won the European Championships. George V started breeding the royal show dogs as well as the pigeons, some of whom nobly saw active service in the Second World War. The kennels now house two of the Queen's favourite breeds, Labradors and corgis.

The Queen and the Duke take a lively interest in the running of their estates and in the wellbeing of those who live and work on them — tenant farmers, keepers, foresters, gardeners, stalkers, craftsmen, and so on. They regularly attend Sunday service in the Sandringham church and the Queen and the Queen Mother both belong to the local Women's Institute.

Balmoral provides perhaps even more seclusion than Sandringham and it is in Scotland that the Royal Family like to spend their longest holiday of the year. Following the example of Queen Victoria, they may stop off on their way to Deeside for a few days at the Palace of Holyroodhouse in Edinburgh to give their Scottish subjects an opportunity to meet them at one of the Queen's garden parties in the grounds. These are magnificently situated below the impressive mound of Arthur's Seat, and the Palace is itself quite a handsome building. Although its history is ancient and sometimes violent — Mary Queen of Scots watched horrified as her Italian secretary Rizzio was murdered at the top of a staircase here — most of today's house is the creation of Charles II and his successors and work on it was not completed until the reign of George V.

Balmoral looks romantically ancient, but it was largely the creation of Queen Victoria's husband, Prince Albert, who transformed the house bought by the couple in the 1850s into the

Above Essentially a countrywoman at heart, the Queen is probably at her happiest with her family in the seclusion of one of her lovely country homes. In February 1982, to celebrate her thirty years on the throne, she was photographed with the Duke of Edinburgh and one of her beloved corgis in the grounds of Sandringham, the Norfolk mansion of which her father was so fond.

Below **Balmoral, the Queen's private Scottish home, was originally the purchase of Prince Albert, husband of Queen Victoria, who enlarged the existing house and gave it the romantic look it has today. During their late summer holiday here the Royal Family like to indulge in a range of outdoor activites – sailing, fishing, riding, shooting and picnicking.**

much larger turreted castle of today. He even went so far as to design his own tartan, named the Balmoral, for the exclusive use of the Royal Family and which made its appearance on the carpets specially woven for the new abode. The grounds of Balmoral provide for today's Royal Family the same range of outdoor pursuits as they did for Queen Victoria's. For those who like sailing and fishing there is Loch Muick and the River Dee, while the moorlands around provide good riding, shooting and deerstalking country. If the weather is good during the August and September retreat a few picnics may be organised in the grounds, with members of the Royal Family doing their own cooking over the hot coals of a barbecue. Harold Wilson has recalled a perfect steak cooked for him by the Queen's own fair hands over a barbecue after she had driven him out in a shooting-brake to one of the cottages on the estate. Balmoral is truly the place where the Queen comes nearest to being just like any other wife and mother, and when she emerges for the nearby Braemar Games there is still somehow a happy family atmosphere about the occasion.

Windsor Castle is of course altogether more formal. It looks what it is, the largest castle in the British Isles. Appearances are in part deceptive for though some of the building dates back to medieval times, much of it, including the distinctive crenellations, was only added in George IV's reign. The Queen has created a comfortable home for her family in the south-east corner of the Upper Ward overlooking the magnificent formal gardens, and it is here that they usually gather for Easter and Ascot week in June as well as for the big Christmas get-together. The Queen does some official entertaining here and customarily reviews the annual parade of Boy Scouts in the Quadrangle at Easter, but she also finds time to exercise her dogs and ride in Windsor Great Park, just as she did as a child, and her husband and oldest son have a chance to pursue their favourite sports of four-in-hand carriage driving and polo.

The happiest time of the year is probably Christmas, a time for relaxation round log fires and for the masses of small children now a part of the family to enjoy the Christmas tree and opening their presents, by tradition a Christmas Eve occupation in royal circles. Christmas Day itself is a day for worship and the scene as the family descend the steps of St George's Chapel is a familiar one.

The Queen's Christmas Day message is nowadays a very sophisticated affair, and pre-recorded, which allows the Queen to relax with her family on Christmas Day in front of the television in much the same way as most of her subjects. Her Christmas Day broadcast remains the most popular programme transmitted during the year, a tribute to the enormous affection and respect still felt for this remarkable lady as she enter her sixties. The family gathering is perhaps bigger than in most families for it includes cousins and their children as well as closer relatives.

Above **Parts of Windsor Castle date back to William the Conqueror's time though it has undergone many changes since then. The Queen has carried out her own alterations to create a comfortable family home in the south-east corner of the Upper Ward overlooking these magnificent formal gardens.**

Opposite, top **Royal Christmases are now spent at Windsor, not Sandringham as in the days of King George VI. There is a large gathering of the royal family, who enjoy such traditional activities as exchanging gifts round the Christmas tree on Christmas Eve and listening to the Queen's Christmas Day speech. In 1984 she delivered it from the Castle's Oak Room and her message of hope and peace was broadcast to over twenty-seven million television viewers.**

Opposite, bottom **Christmas Day 1983 for the Royal Family is one of worship. Before lunch they will have attended two services at St George's Chapel, after one of which there is always a crowd of photographers to catch a view of them as they descend the steps with the Dean.**

Opposite, top, left **On 11 March 1985 the Queen was present at the Commonwealth Day Observance Service at Westminster Abbey.**

Opposite, top, right **In 1985 the educational trust set up to commemorate her grandfather's Silver Jubilee celebrated its Golden Jubilee at St Paul's Cathedral. The Queen is patron of the Trust.**

Opposite, bottom **In February 1985 *Ordeal by Innocence* had its London première in honour of King George's Fund for Sailors, of which the Queen is Patron and Prince Philip President. Stars of the film lined up to meet the Queen and her husband. Among them were Faye Dunaway and Donald Sutherland.**

Below **A glittering figure in white, the Queen arrives at Claridge's for a glittering occasion, the banquet given in her honour by President Banda of Malawi on 18 April 1985.**

Overleaf **The Queen is undoubtedly Britain's best ambassador abroad and in March 1985 made her second state visit to Britain's 'oldest ally', Portugal. The welcome was warm, especially at Oporto where a carpet of camellia petals was strewn in her way.**

The Queen has for so long so manifestly displayed the virtues of humanity, courage, honesty and devotion to duty that even the sternest critics of monarchy can hardly fault her. In spite of the frequent adulation of the multitude she has managed to remain modest and friendly and to keep her sense of humour without in the process devaluing the Crown. As she speaks to peoples around the world from the strength of her position at the centre of a happy and loving family, the Queen sets an example to all of devotion to old-fashioned and basic human virtues, as well as being living fulfilment of that pledge of service made in Cape Town on her coming of age.

INDEX

Entries in *italics* refer to illustrations or information found in captions.

Photographic Acknowledgements

Associated Press, London 186; BBC Hulton Picture Library, London 45 top, 45 bottom, 49, 50, 64 top; BBC Television, London 251 top; Camera Press, London 77; Camera Press: Baron 84–5, 85, 88, 91 bottom right; Camera Press: Cecil Beaton 83, 104–5; Camera Press: Karsh of Ottawa front jacket, 53, 89; Camera Press: Patrick Lichfield 156 bottom, 157, 159, 160, 162–3, 204–5, 225; Camera Press: Lord Snowdon back jacket, 222, 222–3; Tim Graham, London 230–1, 254; Illustrated London News Picture Library, London 36 bottom, 43; Newnes Books 8, 8–9, 9, 10–11, 12–13, 21, 22, 24–5 top, 24–5 bottom, 40 top, 44–5, 46–7, 47, 51 bottom, 58–9, 78, 80 bottom, 108, 108–9, 175, 187, 250; The Photo Source/Central Press, London 6–7, 17, 20, 23 bottom, 26 top, 38, 68, 70, 76 top, 87 top, 90, 94, 96 top, 103; The Photo Source/Colour Library International 79 bottom, 81, 91 top, 107, 155, 172, 199, 208 bottom, 232–3, 248–9; The Photo Source/Fox 18–19 bottom, 27 bottom, 28–9, 29, 33, 34–5 top, 34–5 bottom, 36 top, 37, 40 bottom, 41 top, 41 bottom, 51 top, 52 top left, 56, 57 top, 57 bottom, 60, 60–1, 62–3, 65, 69 bottom, 72, 73, 74–5, 76 bottom, 82,

86–7 top, 86–7 bottom, 91 bottom left, 92, 93, 94–5, 101, 102 right, 102–3, 112, 114 top, 114 bottom, 114–15, 115 left, 115 right, 116–17, 118–19 bottom, 119, 120 top, 123 bottom, 124 bottom, 125, 127, 128 top, 128 bottom, 129 top, 129 bottom, 130–1, 133 top, 133 bottom, 135, 136, 137 top, 137 bottom, 138–9, 139, 140–1 top, 140–1 bottom, 141 bottom, 143, 144 top, 146 right, 148 top, 148 bottom left, 148 bottom right, 149 top left, 149 top right, 149 bottom, 150, 150–1, 151 top, 151 bottom, 152 top, 152 bottom, 152–3, 153 bottom, 154, 161 bottom, 165, 167 top right, 167 bottom, 168, 169 top, 170–1, 171, 184 top, 184 bottom, 185, 188–9 bottom, 189 bottom, 190–1, 192 top, 196 top, 197 top, 200–1 top, 201, 204, 208 top, 209, 211, 213 top left, 214, 215 top, 215 bottom, 217 top, 218–19, 221 top, 221 bottom, 232, 239, 240–1, 247; The Photo Source/Keystone 16, 26 bottom, 27 top, 30–1, 34, 36–7, 39 top, 42, 52 bottom, 54 top, 97; Press Association, London 224; Sport & General Press Agency, London 96 bottom, 110, 111; Syndication International, London frontispiece, 11, 14–15, 18–19 top, 19, 28, 35, 48, 52 top right, 54 bottom, 54–5, 58, 64 bottom, 65 bottom, 66 top, 66 bottom, 66–7, 69 top, 71, 75, 80 top, 84, 87 bottom, 98–9, 100, 102 left, 106 top, 106 bottom, 106–7, 113, 116, 118–19 top, 120 bottom, 121, 122 top, 122 bottom left,

122 bottom right, 123 top left, 123 top right, 124 top, 124–5, 126–7, 132 left, 132 right, 134 left, 134 right, 138 top, 138 bottom, 140, 141 top, 142, 142–3, 144 bottom, 145, 146 left, 147, 153 top, 156 top, 158–9, 161 top, 164, 164–5 top, 164–5 bottom, 166, 167 top left, 169 bottom, 173, 174, 176–7, 178, 179 top, 179 bottom, 180, 181 top, 181 bottom, 182, 182–3 top, 182–3 bottom, 183, 188, 188–9 top, 189 top, 190, 191, 192, 193, 194 top, 194 bottom, 195, 196 bottom, 197 bottom, 198, 200–1 bottom, 202, 202–3, 206, 206–7, 207, 208–9, 210, 210–11, 212, 213 top right, 213 bottom, 214–15 top, 214–15 bottom, 216 top, 216 bottom, 217 centre, 217 bottom, 218, 219 top, 219 bottom, 220, 220–1, 226, 227, 229 top, 229 bottom, 234 top, 234 bottom, 235, 236 top, 236 bottom, 237, 238, 242, 243, 244, 245, 246, 251 bottom, 252 top left, 252 top right, 252 bottom, 253; The Times, London 79 top, 118; Windsor Archives 23 top, 32.